THE PENNSYLVANIA STATE
UNIVERSITY LIBRARIES

ENGINEERING LIBRARY

D1066543

Building Mobile Applications
with Java

Joshua Marinacci

O'REILLY®

Beijing · Cambridge · Farnham · Köln · Sebastopol · Tokyo

Building Mobile Applications with Java
by Joshua Marinacci

Copyright © 2012 Joshua Marinacci. All rights reserved.
Printed in the United States of America.

Published by O'Reilly Media, Inc., 1005 Gravenstein Highway North, Sebastopol, CA 95472.

O'Reilly books may be purchased for educational, business, or sales promotional use. Online editions are also available for most titles (*http://my.safaribooksonline.com*). For more information, contact our corporate/institutional sales department: (800) 998-9938 or *corporate@oreilly.com*.

Editors: Shawn Wallace and Mike Hendrickson	**Cover Designer:** Karen Montgomery	
Production Editor: Teresa Elsey	**Interior Designer:** David Futato	
	Illustrators: Robert Romano and Rebecca Demarest	

Revision History for the First Edition:

    2012-03-08   First release

See *http://oreilly.com/catalog/errata.csp?isbn=9781449308230* for release details.

Nutshell Handbook, the Nutshell Handbook logo, and the O'Reilly logo are registered trademarks of O'Reilly Media, Inc. *Building Mobile Applications with Java*, the image of a pigmy piculet, and related trade dress are trademarks of O'Reilly Media, Inc.

Many of the designations used by manufacturers and sellers to distinguish their products are claimed as trademarks. Where those designations appear in this book, and O'Reilly Media, Inc., was aware of a trademark claim, the designations have been printed in caps or initial caps.

While every precaution has been taken in the preparation of this book, the publisher and authors assume no responsibility for errors or omissions, or for damages resulting from the use of the information contained herein.

ISBN: 978-1-449-30823-0

[LSI]

1331227219

Table of Contents

Preface

I have always thought of Java as a way of coding and an ecosystem, not just a language and virtual machine. When you code in Java you are part of a mature culture with amazing tools and expertise. When I joined the webOS team nearly two years ago I knew HTML and CSS very well, but very little JavaScript. Over time I have become pretty good at JavaScript but my newfound knowledge still can't compare to my fifteen years of mad Java skillz. With Java, and the mature Java tools, I can knock out code in half the time. I didn't want to give up my existing skills to play in the new world of smart devices.

I know I am not the only Java developer facing the job of building cross-platform mobile apps. The Java ecosystem is so big that any solution for using Java in new ways can be immediately used by millions of hard working developers. So I began to research the available options and found GWT and PhoneGap, two brilliant open source projects that let us take Java to new and exciting places. My research turned into a few prototypes, then a few developer talks, a webcast, and finally the book you are reading now.

Even before I began to write I knew I wanted to create a book that was both very hands on and also very short. We are busy people who need tools that work now. We don't have time to spend learning the framework of the week. That meant I had to leave a lot out. GWT is a mature but still growing technology. To truly cover GWT itself would require an entire 500-page book unto itself. To even cover the mobile parts would be beyond what this text could cover. So I decided to focus just on what you need to get started and be productive right away. After reading this book you will be ready to build your own apps and, if you desire, jump into the rich world of third party libraries and tools. The last chapter lists a few to help you get started.

Conventions Used in This Book

The following typographical conventions are used in this book:

Italic
>Indicates new terms, URLs, email addresses, filenames, and file extensions.

Constant width

> Used for program listings, as well as within paragraphs to refer to program elements such as variable or function names, databases, data types, environment variables, statements, and keywords.

Constant width bold

> Shows commands or other text that should be typed literally by the user.

Constant width italic

> Shows text that should be replaced with user-supplied values or by values determined by context.

> This icon signifies a tip, suggestion, or general note.

> This icon indicates a warning or caution.

Using Code Examples

This book is here to help you get your job done. In general, you may use the code in this book in your programs and documentation. You do not need to contact us for permission unless you're reproducing a significant portion of the code. For example, writing a program that uses several chunks of code from this book does not require permission. Selling or distributing a CD-ROM of examples from O'Reilly books does require permission. Answering a question by citing this book and quoting example code does not require permission. Incorporating a significant amount of example code from this book into your product's documentation does require permission.

We appreciate, but do not require, attribution. An attribution usually includes the title, author, publisher, and ISBN. For example: "*Building Mobile Applications with Java* by Joshua Marinacci (O'Reilly). Copyright 2012 Joshua Marinacci, 978-1-449-30823-0."

If you feel your use of code examples falls outside fair use or the permission given above, feel free to contact us at *permissions@oreilly.com*.

Safari® Books Online

 Safari Books Online (*www.safaribooksonline.com*) is an on-demand digital library that delivers expert content in both book and video form from the world's leading authors in technology and business.

Technology professionals, software developers, web designers, and business and creative professionals use Safari Books Online as their primary resource for research, problem solving, learning, and certification training.

Safari Books Online offers a range of product mixes and pricing programs for organizations, government agencies, and individuals. Subscribers have access to thousands of books, training videos, and prepublication manuscripts in one fully searchable database from publishers like O'Reilly Media, Prentice Hall Professional, Addison-Wesley Professional, Microsoft Press, Sams, Que, Peachpit Press, Focal Press, Cisco Press, John Wiley & Sons, Syngress, Morgan Kaufmann, IBM Redbooks, Packt, Adobe Press, FT Press, Apress, Manning, New Riders, McGraw-Hill, Jones & Bartlett, Course Technology, and dozens more. For more information about Safari Books Online, please visit us online.

How to Contact Us

Please address comments and questions concerning this book to the publisher:

O'Reilly Media, Inc.
1005 Gravenstein Highway North
Sebastopol, CA 95472
800-998-9938 (in the United States or Canada)
707-829-0515 (international or local)
707-829-0104 (fax)

We have a web page for this book, where we list errata, examples, and any additional information. You can access this page at:

http://shop.oreilly.com/product/0636920021063.do

To comment or ask technical questions about this book, send email to:

bookquestions@oreilly.com

For more information about our books, courses, conferences, and news, see our website at *http://www.oreilly.com*.

Find us on Facebook: *http://facebook.com/oreilly*

Follow us on Twitter: *http://twitter.com/oreillymedia*

Watch us on YouTube: *http://www.youtube.com/oreillymedia*

Acknowledgments

I would like to thank my editor, Shawn, who has kept this project focused, even as the my own schedule slipped many times due to unexpected events. I would also like to thank my two tech reviewers, Chuq and Cooper, who gave me great feedback and verified my approach. And finally I must thank my wife, Jen, who encouraged me to write even as we are raising our new baby son, Jesse. His will be a world full of rich and fascinating mobile devices. I hope this book will fill them with fun and exciting things.

CHAPTER 1

Greetings, Mobile App Developers

Greetings, welcome, and guten tag. If you've picked up this book, it's probably because you were attracted to the idea of building mobile apps for non-Java platforms with Java. You might not be familiar with GWT and PhoneGap. *That's okay.* I'll explain it all as we go forward. The important thing is that we are here to create great mobile apps.

The actual technology used to build software doesn't really matter to the end user. People just want quality apps that look great and perform well. Unfortunately, the technology *does* matter when it comes down to actually building apps. Different platforms have their own toolchains and preferred languages. iPhone and iPad apps are largely written in Objective-C. Android apps are written in Google's variant of Java. Windows Metro style apps use C#, C++, or Visual Basic. Add in webOS, BlackBerry (both old and new OSes), the Nook (older Android), and Kindle Fire (forked Android), and now we've got a problem.

To support all users we have to write our app at least three times, possibly many more if you count emerging TV platforms. And that's the *good* news. The bad news is that it will only get worse. Mobile platforms are dividing not converging. Even among the Android family there are several major versions in widespread use, and the upgrade rate is sadly low.

So what is an enterprising app developer to do? You want to write an app once, not over and over again. We need a single platform that will work everywhere. Fortunately we already have such a platform: the Web. I'm not speaking about the Web as a network of computers which host HTML content. I'm speaking about the Web technologies HTML, JavaScript, and CSS. Virtually every OS has a web browser, which means it has a way to render HTML and JavaScript. In almost every case there is a way to build a local installable app using HTML and JavaScript. Great! We have a single platform. Problem solved. What now?

Well, if it were that easy we wouldn't need this book. Every OS is different. They each have different support for HTML standards, JavaScript APIs, and native packaging systems. Plus, you would have to write everything in JavaScript rather than the Java code you are likely familiar with. You would have to give up static typing, the large ecosystem of Java libraries, and the great IDE experience we all enjoy. Well, that's why you bought this book.

There are two amazing open source tools which will solve the problem for us: GWT and PhoneGap. GWT allows you to write Java but compile into cross-platform, *works everywhere*, JavaScript and HTML. PhoneGap provides native packaging for each OS, along with API wrappers for device features like the camera, accelerometer, and GPS radio. By their powers combined we can fulfill the dream: write once in a powerful and well supported statically typed language, Java, then produce native apps for every platform with a single codebase. Is the dream too good to be true? As we shall see, it is indeed quite real.

CHAPTER 2

Getting Started with GWT

What Is GWT?

Before we get into building mobile apps let's get to know GWT. GWT, or the Google Web Toolkit, is a set of tools, libraries and plugins. GWT was first released as an open source project by Google in 2006. They built it as a stable platform for their own web based applications that had to run across 100% of browsers, even the old broken ones.

At its core, GWT is a special compiler that can transform Java to JavaScript, along with a minimal runtime. It lets you write mostly standard Java code, then compile it to JavaScript for running in a web browser or other HTML environment. Once compiled there is no Java code left. The generated code runs entirely in the user's web browser as JavaScript, no applets required. GWT has its own runtime consisting of a minimal set of standard Java APIs like List and String. These are implemented in JavaScript so that your code can call them even when converted. You can see the full list of emulated Java APIs at *http://code.google.com/webtoolkit/doc/latest/RefJreEmulation.html*.

GWT isn't just a compiler though. It is also a set of cleverly designed compile steps and runtime libraries that handle browser differences. The compiler can generate different output for each browser, ensuring that the code runs properly no matter what browser the user has, even IE6! The compiler knows how to optimize object references, take advantage of JavaScript language tricks, and reduce memory usage. Much like a traditional compiler it produces code much better than you could write by hand. Even better, the compiler improves over time to take advantage of the evolving browser landscape. Your code will get better without having to rewrite a single line.

Installing GWT

Before we dive into mobile let's build a basic GWT application. First you will need to download the SDK from *http://code.google.com/webtoolkit/download.html*.

You will also need to have Java and Ant installed. If you are a Java developer reading this book then you likely already have these installed. There are special versions of

GWT that work with the popular Java IDE Eclipse, including nice debugger integration. However, since the point of this book is to understand what GWT and PhoneGap are really doing underneath the hood, I won't use anything IDE-specific. Instead I will work with the standalone GWT SDK from the command line. The core SDK is just a set of command line utilities, the jars, and a visual console logger. Just know that once you learn how it really works you may wish to install optimized tools for your favorite IDE or Google's GWT visual designer.

To install GWT, first download the right version for your platform then unzip the gwt-2.4.zip file. The exact filename may be different if you downloaded a version other than 2.4. At the time of this writing, 2.4 was the latest stable version. Move the resulting gwt-2.4.0 directory to wherever you normally work on projects.

From the command line run

```
gwt-2.4.0/webAppCreator -out MyFirstApp com.mycompanyname.MyFirstApp
```

This is the first step to creating any new GWT project. It will generate a new project directory with the package and name specified. It doesn't really matter where you create the project. GWT will set up the correct links between your project and the GWT libs. The webAppCreator will create a new directory filled with a default app. Let's take a quick look at the directory structure:

- MyFirstApp, the directory containing your new app
- MyFirstApp/src contains the Java source for the app. The generated source will use the package name specified above. For example, src/com/mycompanyname/MyFirst App.java
- MyFirstApp/war, the directory containing the web resources for your app. Anything in here will be bundled into a final WAR file for deploying on a Java Servlet Container. (Don't worry, the servlet part isn't required. Hold on a sec). This is where you will put additional images, CSS files, and other web resources.
- MyFirstApp/build.xml An Ant build script to build, test, and compile the app.

To test your app run ant devmode from inside the MyFirstApp directory. This will open the GWT visual logging tool (see Figure 2-1). From here you can launch your desktop web browser, monitor logging, and view exception stack traces. One nice feature of the GWT tool is that it will watch for changes in your code on disk, then recompile and relaunch the app whenever you reload in the browser. This way you can just flip between code and your web browser without any extra compiling or building step.

 The first time you run the tool and launch your browser it will ask you to install a special browser plugin. This plugin creates the link between your browser and the logging tool. I recommend using the Chrome web browser for GWT development as I have found it to provide the best support.

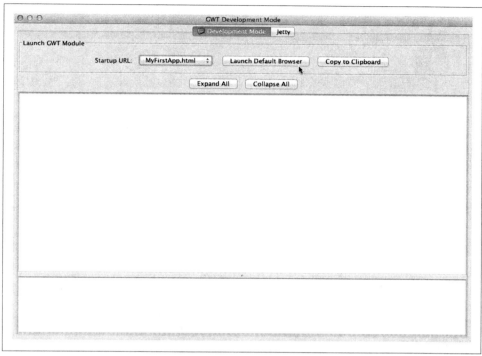

Figure 2-1. GWT development console

The default generated app is pretty simple (Figure 2-2). It has a text field and a button. When you type text into the text field and click the button it will kick off a request to the server and report the results. This is just a demonstration of having both client side and server side GWT components.

Now let's change something and watch the app update.

Open up *src/com/mycompanyname/client/MyFirstApp.java* in your favorite programming editor. If you want a nice pure text editor for coding I recommend the excellent open source JEdit from *jedit.org*. Change the text inside the button to *Greetings Earthling* (it should be on line 41). Save the file. Now switch to your browser and press the reload button. You should see the updated text in the button (Figure 2-3).

Now let's look back at the code to see what it's really doing. Open up *MyFirst-App.java* in your text editor. Pretty much the entire app is contained here. MyFirstApp implements EntryPoint. EntryPoint is a GWT interface defining an onModuleLoad method. This method is called by GWT to start up the app. It is in this method where you create all of your widgets and do other setup. Let's look at the first few lines

```
public void onModuleLoad() {
    final Button sendButton = new Button("Greetings Earthling");
    final TextBox nameField = new TextBox();
```

Figure 2-2. GWT sample project

Figure 2-3. Modified sample project

```
nameField.setText("GWT User");
final Label errorLabel = new Label();
```

GWT uses Java classes to represent widgets on screen. Widgets are UI controls like buttons, panels, drop downs, tables, and lists. The first four lines in the code above create the widgets for this app. The Button class is an on screen button. The TextBox is a single-line text entry field. The Label represents a single line of text. If you have done any Swing programming this will feel very familiar. Notice that the code calls name

Field.setText("gwt user"). GWT follows the Java Beans naming convention so set Text will set the text property of the nameField object.

The next line, addStyleName adds a CSS style class to the widget. Don't worry about this now. We will explore CSS in the mobilization chapter.

```
// We can add style names to widgets
sendButton.addStyleName("sendButton");

// Add the nameField and sendButton to the RootPanel
// Use RootPanel.get() to get the entire body element
RootPanel.get("nameFieldContainer").add(nameField);
RootPanel.get("sendButtonContainer").add(sendButton);
RootPanel.get("errorLabelContainer").add(errorLabel);
```

The last three lines above add the three widgets to objects inside of the root panel. The RootPanel represents the actual web page. The default generated app has a few divs in the web page named *nameFieldContainer*, *sendButtonContainer*, and *errorLabelContainer*. The widgets will be added to these divs. Look at *war/MyFirstApp.html* to see the divs.

You don't have to use prefab divs in your HTML, though. You could instead add them directly to the root panel or nest them inside of another panel. For example, if you wanted to put the widgets in a vertical panel, where the widgets are all arranged in a vertical column, you could do it like this:

```
VerticalPanel vertPanel = new VerticalPanel();
vertPanel.add(nameField);
vertPanel.add(sendButton);
vertPanel.add(errorLabel);
RootPanel.get().add(vertPanel);
```

Notice that I changed RootPanel.get("somename") to RootPanel.get(). This will get the root panel itself instead of one of the nested divs.

GWT supports mapping into parts of the markup or taking over the entire page. This gives you a choice of how to build your application. For mobile apps I prefer to take over the entire page and only use markup and CSS for styling.

The next few lines of *MyFirstApp.java* make the name field be focused when the user first opens the web page, then selects all of the text within the name field. This means the user will overwrite the selected text when they start typing.

```
// Focus the cursor on the name field when the app loads
nameField.setFocus(true);
nameField.selectAll();
```

The rest of the MyFirstApp class creates a remote procedure call to the server, then displays the results in a dialog box. I won't cover this part because we will never be using GWT's own remote procedure call system in this book. GWT was originally designed to be run on Java EE app servers. It will generate both server and client side components with a nice mapping between them. For our apps, however, we are only interested in the client part, which is the part that will actually be installed on to the device. If you write an app which does some server communication to your own server then you may find GWT's server side infrastructure useful. I have found that I prefer to use generic server infrastructure that serves up standard XML or JSON rather than something specific to GWT. It's really up to you what you should use.

Though I'm skipping the remote procedure call stuff I want to point your attention to line 79: *closeButton.addClickHandler()*. GWT has event listeners for the different widgets. Buttons can receive click events. To do something when the click happens you must add a ClickHandler to the button. That is what the code below does.

```
// Add a handler to close the DialogBox
closeButton.addClickHandler(new ClickHandler() {
  public void onClick(ClickEvent event) {
    dialogBox.hide();
    sendButton.setEnabled(true);
    sendButton.setFocus(true);
  }
});
```

It creates an anonymous implementation of ClickHandler, then adds it to the button. When the user clicks on the button the onClick method of the handler will be called. Put whatever code you want to be executed inside the onClick method. In the code above it hides the dialog box and enables the sendButton.

The various Handler interfaces in GWT are similar to the Listener pattern used in Swing and other standard Java GUI toolkits. There is one important difference, though: there is no `removeClickHandler` method. All addHandler methods return a HandlerRegistration object with a `removeHandler()` method. This makes it very easy to manage your listeners. Just dump the registration objects into an array list somewhere. When you are ready to shut down your app, or a component, loop through the list and call removeHandler() on all of the objects. This will clean up your memory without having to know which listeners when to which object.

Building a Twitter Search App

Now that we know how GWT works let's build our own small app called PerchSearch. It will be a simple one screen app to search for Twitter tweets containing a particular keyword. This app will do basic networking, have a text field and button, and a list of labels for the tweets. Once we have the app working we can restyle it to look a bit better on a mobile device.

To build the app I first created a new project like this:

```
gwt-2.4.0/webAppCreator -out PerchSearch com.joshondesign.perchsearch.PerchSearch
```

Then I deleted most of the generated code in *PerchSearch.java*, leaving an empty class like this:

```
public class PerchSearch implements EntryPoint {
    public void onModuleLoad() {
    }
}
```

The app needs a text field for the user to type in a search term, a button to start the search, an error label, and a panel to store the results. To keep things simple let's put them one below the next in a vertical panel.

```
final TextBox queryField = new TextBox();
final VerticalPanel resultsPanel = new VerticalPanel();

public void onModuleLoad() {
    VerticalPanel panel = new VerticalPanel();

    queryField.setText("puppy");
    panel.add(queryField);

    final Button searchButton = new Button("Search Twitter");
    panel.add(searchButton);

    final Label errorLabel = new Label();
    panel.add(errorLabel);

    panel.add(resultsPanel);

    RootPanel.get().add(panel);

    searchButton.addClickHandler(new TwitterHandler());
}
```

The last line adds a custom click handler, TwitterHandler, to the search button. This handler will do the actual API call to Twitter and process the results.

Calling Twitter with JSONP

Twitter provides a JSON API to search for recent tweets based on keywords. When you request a specific URL with a keyword Twitter will return the list of tweets as a JSON file.

JSON, or JavaScript Object Notation, is a way of encoding data as light weight Java-Script arrays and hashtables. For example, a list of first and last names might look like this:

```
[
    { "first":"Jon", "last":"Stewart" },
    { "first":"Jason", "last":"Jones" },
    { "first":"Samantha", "last":"Bee" },
]
```

If you call the URL *http://search.twitter.com/search.json?q=puppy* you will get back a very long list that looks like this:

```
{"completed_in":0.166,"max_id":141224447708364801,
...

"results":[
  {"created_at":"Mon, 28 Nov 2011 18:38:26 +0000",
   "from_user":"foobar","from_user_id":098709874523,
  "text":"I love my puppy"},
  {"created_at":"Mon, 28 Nov 2011 18:38:24 +0000",
   "from_user":"misterman","from_user_id":445388888,
  "text":"My puppy rolled around on the floor. },
  ...
```

In short, you get a giant blob of structured data. I've trimmed it down a bit to make it easier to understand. From this blob we can easily pull out the parts we want. There's a problem, though; we can't actually request this API from a web page.

For security reasons a web page can only make a network request to the server that the web page came from. Since our app will not live on any server, but rather on the end user's device, we can't make a request to anywhere! To get around this limitation enterprising developers invented something called JSONP. JSONP is the same as JSON except the server wraps the result in a call to a method that is defined in the page. This is called a *callback* method. Instead of loading the request directly using something like XmlHttpRequest, it will use the URL as JavaScript source code to be added to the top of the page like this:

```
<script src="http://search.twitter.com/search.json?q=puppy&callback=mycallback"></
script>
```

This essentially tricks the browser into making the API call in the guise of loading source, which *is* allowed by the security model, then invoking your callback method with the resulting data. It sounds a bit tricky, and it is actually, but we don't have to worry about it. GWT handles all of the details for us using a nice class called the *JsonpRequestBuilder*. You just give it a URL and a callback, GWT does the rest. Here's what the code looks like.

```
class TwitterHandler implements ClickHandler {
    public void onClick(ClickEvent event) {
        String url = "http://search.twitter.com/search.json?q="+queryField.getText();
        JsonpRequestBuilder jsonp = new JsonpRequestBuilder();
        jsonp.requestObject(url, new AsyncCallback<JavaScriptObject>() {
                public void onFailure(Throwable throwable) {
                    System.out.println("Error: " + throwable);
                }
                public void onSuccess(JavaScriptObject o) {
                    ...
                }
        });
    }
};
```

I know it looks a bit hairy but it is actually pretty straight forward. The URL is defined in *url* then it creates a new *JsonpRequestBuilder*. It calls *requestObject* using the URL and an anonymous *AsyncCallback* object. When the callback succeeds it will call *on-Success* with a *JavaScriptObject*. With this object in hand we can start pulling out the parts we want.

If you look at the raw output of the Twitter API call in your browser you can paw through it to find what you want. The raw output can be difficult to read so you might want to use a JSON formatter like: *http://jsonformatter.curiousconcept.com/*.

The list of tweets is an array stored with the *results* key. Within each tweet we want the *text* property, which contains the actual text of the tweet. The code to process the list looks like this:

```
JSONObject js = new JSONObject(o);
JSONArray results = js.get("results").isArray();
resultsPanel.clear();
for(int i=0; i<results.size(); i++) {
    String text = (results.get(i).isObject()).get("text").toString();
    Label label = new Label(text);
    resultsPanel.add(label);
}
```

For each item in the results it adds a new Label with the text to the resultsPanel. Notice the call to resultsPanel.clear() before the loop. This removes the old labels before adding new ones.

This is what the final app looks like in the web browser (Figure 2-4). You can get the full source from the book's web page.

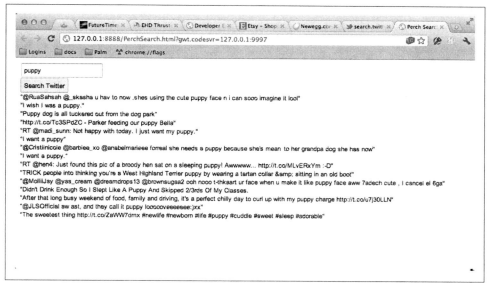

Figure 2-4. PerchSearch searching for the keyword "puppy"

Not the prettiest app in the world, but it works quite well, and with very little code. Go ahead and try it. Type in *puppy* to see what cute things people are saying about puppies. Now type in *lolcat* to have more fun. Yeah, that's better.

Next Steps

We have used GWT to build an app which runs in a web browser. To run it on a mobile device we could just load it up in the mobile browser. However, this won't feel very much like a native app. It won't have an icon or live in the device's app launcher. Also the app itself will look ugly and hard to read on a smaller mobile screen. In the next chapter we will look at a tool to convert the web page into a real app that looks and feels right on a mobile device.

CHAPTER 3

Getting Started with PhoneGap

PhoneGap is an open source collection of build scripts and native wrappers for multiple mobile platforms. PhoneGap generates a native executable from your app for each platform it supports. This native executable is code which can actually be installed on a real device as a native app. The end users will never know that you coded it in JavaScript rather than Objective C or whatever the native SDK uses. For iOS devices it will be an Objective C Xcode project. For Android it will be an Android stub app written in Java. For webOS the apps are mostly HTML already so PhoneGap provides a simple make file to assemble the app. On each platform the native wrapper will open an embedded HTML renderer (usually called a *web view*) to run the rest of your app.

PhoneGap also provides a set of consistent JavaScript hooks to native APIs like the accelerometer, camera, and GPS. These are APIs which typically aren't available when running as a web page loaded from the Internet. PhoneGap wraps the native APIs to provide a consistent cross-device platform for you to code against. This means you can access device features while only having to write your app once.

PhoneGap is an open source project started by the team at Nitobi, hosted at *http:// phonegap.com/*. During the writing of this book Adobe began to use PhoneGap as a component in some of their tools, then eventually bought the Nitobi company and transferred official ownership of PhoneGap to Apache. The transition to Apache is currently in progress and may be complete by the time you read this. As part of the Apache Foundation, PhoneGap will gain even more features and community support under its new name: Apache Cordova.

PhoneGap has three major advantages over direct platform coding:

1. You can code using HTML and JavaScript rather than the native language.
2. You can use the same code and APIs across all platforms.
3. You can code using web technology but still have the app run locally and offline, unlike a pure web app loaded from a remote server.

Packaging a webOS App

Let's start learning how to use PhoneGap by turning our Twitter app from the previous chapter into a native webOS app. I've chosen webOS as the first example because it is the easiest to get started with on any platform, and all of the tools are free. It involves the least transformation from original code to native executable, so it will be easier to debug as well. From there we will move on to Android and iOS.

Installing the webOS SDK

First, download and install VirtualBox from:

https://www.virtualbox.org/

then the webOS SDK from:

https://www.virtualbox.org/

You need VirtualBox because webOS's emulator is really just an x86 build of the entire OS distributed as a VirtualBox image. This makes it very easy to manage multiple versions of the OS: just switch images. Leveraging VirtualBox also means you can do webOS development on Mac, Windows, or Linux. Since it is a real OS emulator rather than a simulator it will give you a better idea of how the app will work on a real device. You can even install apps directly into the emulator from the command line.

Now download the newest version of PhoneGap from:

http://phonegap.com/

Version 1.2 is the latest release as of the time of this writing. You will download a ZIP file containing a bunch of directories, one for each platform. For the webOS app make a copy of the webOS directory and rename it to *PerchSearch-webos*. Start the webOS emulator. From the command line go to the *PerchSearch-webos* directory and run:

```
make
```

This will build the default webOS app and launch it in the emulator. You should see the default app come up in the emulator. It will look like Figure 3-1.

Building PerchSearch for webOS

The PhoneGap app structure is pretty simple. It has a copy of PhoneGap (with scripts to build it) and a directory called framework/ The contents of your app go in there. The GWT app we created put its generated code in PerchSearch/war. Copy everything from the PerchSearch/war into +framework/.

Now open the framework/appinfo.json file and change main to point to Perch-Search.html.

```
"main": "PerchSearch.html",
```

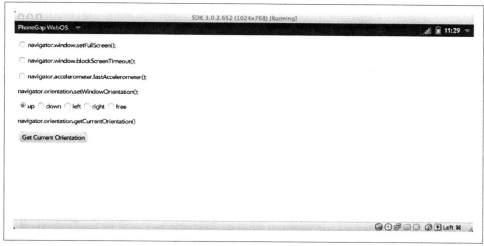

Figure 3-1. Default PhoneGap app in the webOS emulator

Now edit `PerchSearch.html` to add a script tag that will load PhoneGap. Put it right before the line that loads `perchseach.nocache.js`.

```
<script type="text/javascript" language="javascript" src="phonegap-1.0.0.js"></script>
<script type="text/javascript" language="javascript" src="perchsearch/
perchsearch.nocache.js"></script>
```

Now run `make` again and you should see the app pop up in the emulator (Figure 3-2).

Figure 3-2. PerchSearch running in the webOS emulator

That's all you have to do to make a GWT app run on webOS. PhoneGap takes care of assembling the final webOS app, packaging it into an IPK file, and installing it in the emulator. If you had a real webOS device attached to your computer via USB (and the device was in Developer Mode) then it would launch on the real device instead.

You will probably want to customize your app, such as changing the name from the default. You can do this by editing the `framework/www/appinfo.json` file. This file contains most of the metadata for a webOS app. Change the `id` line to use the package name of your app. Change the `vendor` to your name or company. Leave type as `web`. (webOS has other kinds of apps besides web based ones). And finally change the title to the "PerchSearch".

You can also change the icon by replacing `icon.png` with your own 64×64 pixel PNG-encoded icon. You may need to delete and reinstall the app from the webOS emulator to see the updated icon in the webOS app launcher screen.

My final *appinfo.json* file looks like this:

```
{
        "id": "com.phonegap.webos",
        "version": "0.0.1",
        "vendor": "Palm",
        "type": "web",
        "main": "index.html",
        "title": "PhoneGap WebOS",
        "uiRevision": 2
}
```

Debugging Your webOS App

If there are problems with the webOS version of your app you will want to debug it. First, try to fix any issues through the browser rather than on webOS. The browser will always have far superior HTML debugging capabilities, especially when coupled with the GWT plugin.

Once you have exhausted the capabilities of using your desktop browser you can try running the app in your mobile browser. Remember, it's just a fancy web page so the mobile browser can run 99% of it. You may want to turn on advanced logging, including an on-screen console. You can do this by editing *PerchSearch.gwt.xml* and adding the following lines:

```
<!-- logging setup -->
<inherits name="com.google.gwt.logging.Logging"/>
<set-property name="gwt.logging.logLevel" value="ALL"/>
<set-property name="gwt.logging.popupHandler" value="ENABLED" />
```

This will let you view the log messages from the GWT console or on-screen. If the problem really is on the JavaScript side, say a bug in PhoneGap itself, then you can use webOS's own logging system. Once the app is running you can view the log remotely using `palm-log -f com.foo.bar.myapp`. This is similar to the Unix command *tail*. It will follow the log file on (the device or emulators') disk in your terminal. This will print the actual JavaScript errors with line numbers.

Packaging an Android App

Running your GWT app on Android is very similar to the process we used for webOS. First you need to download the Android SDK, which includes the command line tools, GUI tools, and its own device simulator. Download the correct SDK for your platform from this page:

http://developer.android.com/sdk/index.html

Unzip the download and put it wherever you store your tools. This SDK app is actually a shell which lets you manage multiple versions of the Android SDK. You will need to run the `android` application in the `tools` directory to launch this shell and pick the version of the Android platform you want to work with. I chose Android 4.0, which is the latest version released for phones. You need to install both the SDK and the ARM API for your desired Android release.

If you have any troubles I suggest following Google's Android excellent quick start guide:

http://developer.android.com/sdk/installing.html

Setting Up the Android Emulator

Note: if you have trouble downloading with HTTPS (perhaps due to some proxy in the way) you can change the settings in the GUI to use HTTP instead.

To test an app you must set up the Android emulator (Figure 3-3). The SDK comes with its own emulator based on QEMU, but you must set it up before you run it the first time. Run the graphical Android tool called `android` in the `sdk/tools` directory then create a new virtual device. Select the menu item Tools→Manage AVDs...

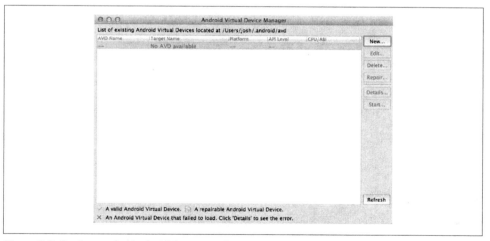

Figure 3-3. Setting up the Android device emulator

Pick a name for your new virtual device, something like *phonegap_tester*. The name must not have spaces. Choose the SDK you've installed and leave the defaults for the rest of the options. Then click `create avd` to create the virtual device. Now you can launch the emulator (Figure 3-4). For example, from the command line run `./emulator @phonegap_tester` if you named your virtual device `phonegap_tester`.

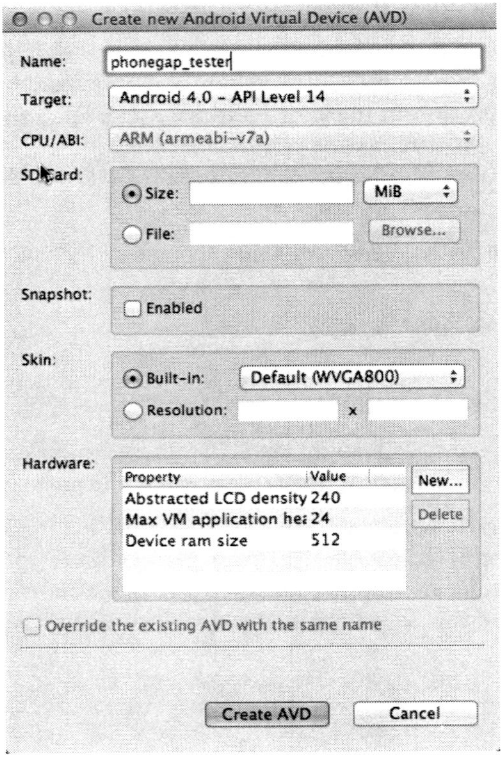

Figure 3-4. Create new Android emulator

It will take a while to boot up since it is emulating the entire Android OS and device hardware. Once it's booted you can compile and run your apps in the emulator (Figure 3-5).

PerchSearch for Android

Similar to what we did for webOS, copy the Android/Sample directory from where you saved PhoneGap to your development directory (probably next to where you put the `phonegap-palm` directory). Rename the directory to something like `perchsearch-android`.

Figure 3-5. Android Emulator running

Now you need to let the project know where you have installed the android SDK and choose the version of the API you want. You do this by running the following command:

```
android update project --path <project path> --target <android version>
```

I have downloaded the Android 4.0.3 SDK, so I will use the target release of android-15. You can see a list of installed releases with

```
android list targets
```

For example, on my computer I did this:

```
~/bin/android-sdk-macosx/tools/android update project --path perchsearch-android --
target android-15
```

Now go into the project directory and build and install the application into the emulator with

```
ant clean debug install
```

This command will fully build the app and install it in the emulator but it will not actually launch the app. Instead you must manually go to the emulator and click on the app's icon to start it. Sometimes `ant install` will fail to find the emulator. If that happens just run it again. Now you should have the standard PhoneGap app running in the Android emulator (Figure 3-6). If `ant clean debug install` failed to actually install the app then try restarting the emulator and run it again.

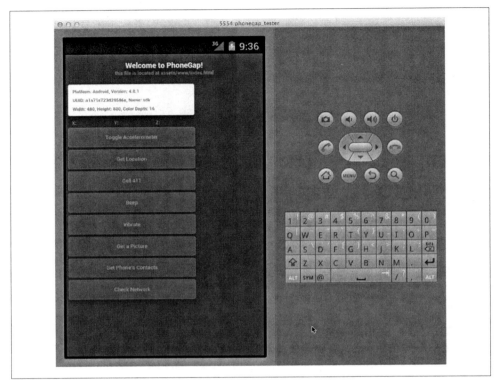

Figure 3-6. PhoneGap running in Android emulator

To make our own app ready for Android we do the same thing we did with webOS: copy the contents of *PerchSearch/war/* to the `perchsearch-android/assets/www` directory. Also rename PerchSearch.html to index.html. To rebuild the app run `ant clean debug install` again. Each time you change your source code you will need to copy it over to the *www* directory and recompile. The app looks like Figure 3-7 in the Android emulator.

Note: If the plain PhoneGap template works but your app loads only as a white screen in the Android emulator then you may have stumbled across a new bug. In Android 4+ the webkit implementation introduced a new security feature that can break apps which use iframe. By default GWT will use an iframe as part of the generated code. Disable this by adding `<add-linker name="xs" />` to your gwt.xml file and recompile the GWT project. Now it should work in Android 4+.

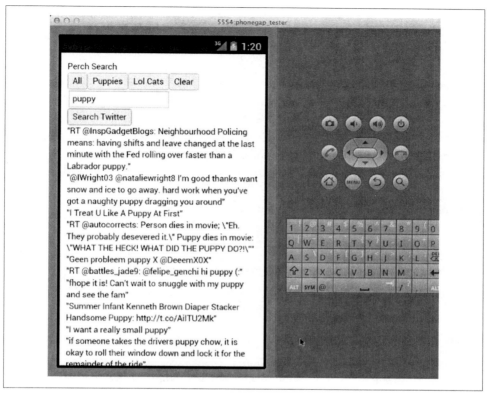

Figure 3-7. PerchSearch running in the Android emulator

You can view the debugging log with this command:

```
~/bin/android-sdk-macosx/platform-tools/adb logcat
```

Packaging an iOS App

Packaging a GWT app for iOS is similar to what we did for webOS and Android. You need the native iOS development tools, Xcode, as well as the latest version of Phone Gap, which includes a special template for building iOS apps. Xcode is Apple's C/C++/Objective-C IDE. It only runs on Mac OS X so you will need a Mac to compile and build iOS apps.

Installing Xcode and PhoneGap

Apple recently moved all of their downloads into the Mac App store, so you can easily get Xcode for free from there. If you don't have the Mac App store client installed you can get installation instructions on *http://www.apple.com/*. You will need the latest version of Snow Leopard or Lion (Mac OS X 10.6 or 10.7). When you download Xcode it won't actually download Xcode itself but rather a giant installer bundle which you will need to run once to really install Xcode. Previously you had to install the iOS SDK separately, but it is now built into Xcode 4.

Next open the `PhoneGap-1.3.0.dmg` file that came with your PhoneGap download and run the `PhoneGap-1.3.0.pkg` installer. This will build and run PhoneGap's own Xcode installer to put PhoneGap templates into Xcode. You only need to do this step once. Now you are ready to build a new Xcode project.

Start Xcode and select File → New Project. Under the iOS "Application" section choose the `PhoneGap-based Application` icon and click next. Now enter a name for your application (Product Name) and Company Identifier. I used "PerchSearch for iPhone" and "Josh On Design."

Right click on *PerchSearch for iPhone* in the left hand Project navigator view. Select *Add Files to "PerchSearch for iPhone…."* Choose the *www* directory from the file chooser and make sure *create folder references for any added folders* is selected. Then click *add*. This will add the *www* directory to your project. This directory already has a simple PhoneGap project in it so now you can click the *run* button in the upper left to run it. The iPhone simulator should start and you should see the default PhoneGap app. Now we can bring over the GWT code.

PerchSearch for iOS

This goes just like before. Copy the contents of *PerchSearch/var* to the *www* directory of your new iPhone project. Press `build` and `run`. It should look like Figure 3-8.

It looks just like we expect. Now try typing into the search box. You will see the iPad keyboard come up automatically. But when you press the search button nothing happens. This exact same code runs fine in the web browser so there must be a particular issue with the iPad. Let's figure out why.

In the View menu of Xcode select the Navigators → Show Log Navigator menu option or press command 7. The left hand pane will switch to show the list of recent log files. Click on the first item in the list. This will show the most recent log file in the main menu. The log shows a few warning messages about PerchSearch then an error that looks like this

```
2011-12-30 11:11:45.377 PerchSearch for iPhone[13595:15503] ERROR whitelist rejection:
url='http://search.twitter.com/search.json?
q=puppy&callback=__gwt_jsonp__.P0.onSuccess'
```

As it turns out iOS will not let apps arbitrarily access any site on the web. iOS apps use a whitelist to ensure only valid sites are accessed. You can add twitter.com to the whitelist by opening up the PerchSearch for *iPhone/Supporting Files/PhoneGap.plist* file in the Xcode sidebar. Then add a new entry under the *External Hosts* section. Insert * `twitter.com`, without any http or leading dot. It will look like Figure 3-9.

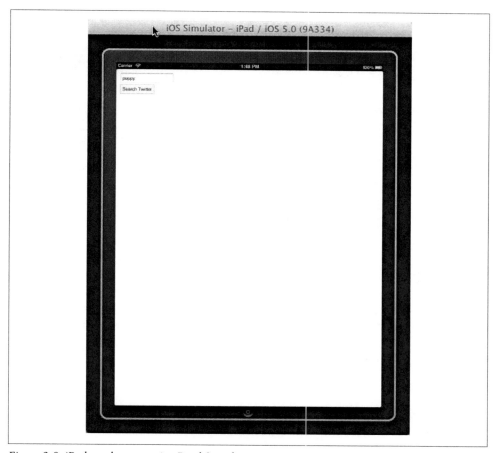

Figure 3-8. iPad emulator running PerchSearch

Now do a clean build (Product → Clean) then run the app again. This time the twitter search will work.

Congratulations! You have now ported a GWT app to webOS, Android and iOS. Updating the code for each project is simple: after making changes to your GWT project build it with `ant build` then copy the contents of *PerchSearch/war* to the appropriate www directory of each project. That's all there is to it.

For each platform PhoneGap will build a native executable or package which can be installed on an emulator, a real device, and submitted to that platform's app store.

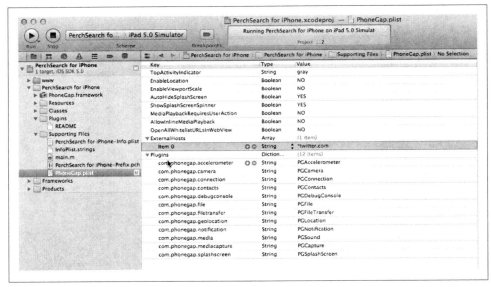

Figure 3-9. Figure editing the PhoneGap.plist file

CHAPTER 4

Customizing Your App for Mobile

So far we have gotten our example app onto a mobile device, but that doesn't really make it *ready for mobile*. Mobile devices are different than desktop computers. Not only do they have smaller screens but they are also usually touch driven. Fingers are bigger than a mouse cursor. Certain actions, like scrolling, are easier to do with a finger, whereas other actions like opening drop down menus are harder or impossible to do without a mouse.

Finally, mobile devices typically have a slower network connection and less processing power than a full blown desktop or laptop. You must take all of these complications into account in order to create a great mobile experience, and that is before we even consider mobile specific features like GPS and accelerometers.

In this section we will take a look at the ways mobile devices are different and how to adapt content and applications to these new constraints.

CSS Overview

Fundamentally GWT builds apps with the technology of web pages. Even though we almost never have to touch the HTML markup directly, GWT is using HTML, Java-Script, and CSS underneath. Most modern web sites use HTML only to represent the content of a page or application. The visuals and styling are controlled using a separate document called a Cascading Style Sheet, or CSS file. A CSS file controls the drawing of each element on the screen. It controls both *how* it is drawn: the colors, backgrounds, fonts, and effects; as well as *where* it is drawn: the layout and sizing. CSS is a powerful technology that can completely transform HTML content for different target devices.

As a quick review, here is what CSS looks like:

```
div {
    font-size: 200%;
}

div.foo {
```

```
    color: blue;
  }
```

A CSS file consists of a list of rules. Each rule has two parts: the *selector* and the *properties*. The selector determines what the rule affects. The selector `div` will apply the rule only to `div` elements. A selector of `div.foo` will apply the rule only to divs with a css class of "foo". For example:

```
<div> not affected by div.foo </div>
<div class="foo"> *IS* affected by div.foo </div>
```

The second part of a CSS rule is the list of property settings. A property is some attribute of an element, such as its color, font, width, or background image. Different elements support different properties and in different ways, though mostly this will be hidden for us by GWT.

The combination of selectors and properties let us style any element in any way we choose with a very compact syntax. For example: to color all text inside of a bold element b with red and give it a solid one-pixel black border, we can use this style:

```
b {
    color: red;
    border: 1px solid black;
}
```

Styling GWT with CSS

So how does this apply to GWT? Remember that every GWT widget ultimately becomes an element in a web page, usually a DIV. GWT helpfully adds CSS style classes to every widget based on that widget's Java class name. With this style class we can hang any style we want.

Suppose we want to make every text field in the app have a thick green border. We can do this with the following style:

```
.gwt-TextBox {
  border: 5px solid green;
}
```

Now that we have the mechanics of CSS working, let's use CSS to restyle PerchSearch from last chapter.

To demonstrate the power of CSS I added a bit more to the UI of the PerchSearch app from the previous chapter. I added a header at the top and a navigation bar on the side. If I load it directly onto a 1024×768 tablet, it looks like Figure 4-1.

The basic UI is functional but ugly. Fortunately we can easily add some style. First I added style names to the header, sidebar, and labels for each tweet using the `addStyle Name` method on the widgets.

```
//in the init code
header.addStyleName("header");
```

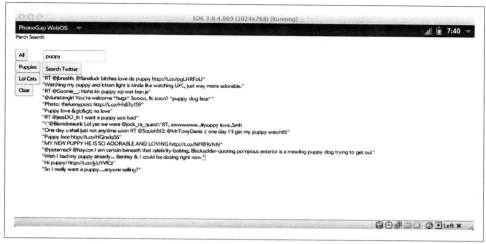

Figure 4-1. Functional but ugly default UI

```
...
nav.addStyleName("nav");
...
//in the tweet handler onSuccess callback
label.addStyleName("tweet");
```

Now we can hang some style on the UI. I want the header to be larger and centered. The navigation buttons should be plain blue with white text instead of the standard button look. The actual tweet text should be bigger with a more spacing and subtle border. To do all of this I added the following code to the `PerchSearch.css` file in the war directory.

```css
.header {
    font-size: 200%;
    text-align: center;
}

.nav .gwt-Button {
    width: 100%;
    margin: 3px 0px 3px 0px;
    color: white;
    background: none;
    background-color: rgb(160,200,250);
    border: 0px solid black;
}

.tweet {
    color: black;
    padding: 0.3em;
    font-size: 130%;
    margin: 2px;
    border: 1px solid #e0e0e0;
```

```
    background-color: #fafafa;
}
```

Notice the buttons are styled with the selector .nav .gwt-Button. This is a compound selector. It means that the properties will only affect elements marked with gwt-But ton that are *also* inside of an element marked with nav. This restricts the style changes to only the navigation buttons. The button next to the text field won't be affected.

The final result is in Figure 4-2.

Figure 4-2. The reskinned interface

Adapting to Device Screen Sizes

The next consideration for any mobile app is screen size. Mobile devices have smaller screens with higher DPI than desktop monitors and they are usually viewed closer to the eye than a desktop. To account for this the web browser on most smart phones assumes a screen width of 960 pixels rather than the actual pixel width of the device (for example, 320px in portrait mode on the original iPhone). The browser allows the user to zoom in and out of the screen dynamically. This is great for random pages on the web but for a mobile app you want greater control over how the user sees your content.

The first adjustment we can make is to force the page to render at the same size as the physical screen. We can do this by adding a meta tag to the `head` section of the page. For a GWT app this means adding the following to the `war/PerchSearch.html` file.

```
<meta name="viewport" content="width=device-width; initial-scale=1.0;
    user-scalable=no;" />
```

By setting `width=device-width` it will tell the browser to make one pixel on your page equal one real pixel on the device. The third command, `user-scalable=no`, disables user scaling. Since we have the page at exactly the right width the user shouldn't have to scale. Instead we will make our text the right size for a mobile device. This only disables *scaling*, though. The user can still pan around. However, as long as we make sure there is no content sticking off the edge page the user will only need to pan up and down, which is the easiest gesture for a mobile device with a touch screen.

So far we have restyled PerchSearch to run on a tablet at 1024×768, which is close enough to a desktop to work in both places. However, if we put it on a standard iPhone in portrait mode then we will have only 320 pixels across to work with. It will look like Figure 4-3.

Not horrible but the sidebar really takes away from the tweets. We could change the fonts and layout to work on the phone, but then it would look wrong on the tablet again. We need a way to specify style for each device, preferably without hard coding it to specific brands of devices.

Fortunately CSS has a solution: media selectors. You can designate a block of CSS rules to apply only to a particular size of screen. For example, if we want to make the fonts smaller on a phone but larger on a tablet we can use this CSS.

```
@media screen and (max-width: 1024px) {
    .header {
        font-size: 200%;
    }
}
@media screen and (max-width: 320px) {
    .header {
        font-size: 120%;
    }
}
.header {
    text-align:center;
}
```

The beauty of this approach is that the browser will ignore anything that doesn't match the current device. If you are on a phone then the rules in the 320px block will override the rules from the 1024px block. If you are on a tablet then you will get the 1024px block and the 320px block will be completely ignored. The `text-align` rule is not inside any block so it will always apply.

Figure 4-3. PerchSearch running on iOS

CSS media queries support conditions based on width, height, orientation, aspect ratio, and other device features. (See the full CSS spec here for details *http://www.w3.org/TR/css3-mediaqueries/*). Using media queries lets you completely customize the look of your app for each device size without changing your actual app code at all, and again it degrades gracefully on older devices.

Adjusting Layout for Mobile

Now that leads us into the next problem: layout. It is very common to create websites which have two or three columns. The left and right columns usually have navigation or sidebars while the center column contains the same information. Squishing this onto a mobile screen is never going to look good, as we can see on the iPhone screenshot. The user will either have to zoom out to see everything or pan to the left and right to see the navigation.

A better solution is to change the layout dynamically to fit the device. You can use the traditional three column layout on a desktop, but switch to two columns (nav + content) for a tablet and one column on a phone, putting the navigation and sidebar above or below the content. Thanks to CSS media selectors we can do this entirely with our style sheets, not changing the app code at all.

To adjust PerchSearch for a phone sized device we will make it fit into one column by moving the navigation to be between the header and content. To not waste vertical space we will also make the navigation be horizontal. To determine which CSS to use we need to know what markup GWT has generated for us.

If you use a desktop web browser with a page inspector like Chrome you can see the generated markup. The markup for the main DockLayoutPanel of PerchSearch looks like this:

```
<div style="position: absolute; left: 0px; top: 0px; right: 0px; bottom: 0px; "><div
style="position: absolute; z-index: -32767; top: -20ex; width: 10em; height: 10ex;
"> </div><div style="position: absolute; overflow-x: hidden; overflow-y: hidden;
left: 0px; top: 0px; right: 0px; bottom: 0px; "><div style="position: absolute; left:
0px; right: 0px; top: 0px; bottom: 0px; " class="dock"><div style="position: absolute;
z-index: -32767; top: -20ex; width: 10em; height: 10ex; "> </div><div
style="position: absolute; overflow-x: hidden; overflow-y: hidden; left: 0em; top:
0em; right: 0em; height: 3em; "><div class="gwt-Label header" style="position:
absolute; left: 0px; right: 0px; top: 0px; bottom: 0px; ">PerchSearch</div></div><div
style="position: absolute;    left: 0em; top: 3em; bottom: 0em; width: 5em; "><div
class="nav" style="position: absolute; left: 0px; right: 0px; top: 0px; bottom: 0px;
"><button type="button" class="gwt-Button">All</button><button type="button"
class="gwt-Button">Puppies</button><button type="button" class="gwt-Button">Lol Cats</
button><button type="button" class="gwt-Button">Clear</button></div></div><div
style="position: absolute; overflow-x: hidden; overflow-y: hidden; left: 5em; top:
3em; right: 0em; bottom: 0em; "><table cellspacing="0" cellpadding="0"
style="position: absolute; left: 0px; right: 0px; top: 0px; bottom: 0px;
"><tbody><tr><td align="left" style="vertical-align: top; "><input type="text"
class="gwt-TextBox"></td></tr><tr><td align="left" style="vertical-align: top;
"><button type="button" class="gwt-Button">Search Twitter</button></td></tr><tr><td
align="left" style="vertical-align: top; "><div class="gwt-Label"></div></td></
tr><tr><td align="left" style="vertical-align: top; "><table cellspacing="0"
cellpadding="0"><tbody></tbody></table></td></tr></tbody></table></div></div></div></
div>
```

Uh oh. That's not good. DockLayoutPanel generates many extra divs with lots of inline styles. That's going to be very hard to override with CSS. We need another solution.

To tackle this problem we will use a technique called "tags first GWT". For some applications you don't care about the markup and can use whatever GWT generates. For other applications, like mobile ones, we want to specify *some* of the markup first, then tell GWT to work with what we created. GWT does this very easily using the RootPanel.

Normally we call RootPanel.get().add(panel) to add a panel to the root of the page. RootPanel optionally lets us specify an id of the HTML element we want to use instead of defaulting to the root of the page. With this technique we can insert GWT markup inside of our own custom page.

Let's start by modifying the main app page in `war/PerchSearch.html`. Previously the body was empty. Now let's create our own set of divs, one for each major chunk of the app.

```
<div id="dock_container">
    <div id="header_container"></div>
    <div id="nav_container"></div>
    <div id="content_container"></div>
</div>
```

Now modify the Java code to use these nice clean divs. First I removed all references to the dock panel.

```
Label header = new Label("PerchSearch");
header.addStyleName("header");

FlowPanel nav = new FlowPanel();
nav.add(new Button("All"));
nav.add(new Button("Puppies"));
nav.add(new Button("Lol Cats"));
nav.add(new Button("Clear"));
nav.addStyleName("nav");

VerticalPanel panel = new VerticalPanel();
panel.addStyleName("content");
queryField.setText("puppy");
panel.add(queryField);
final Button searchButton = new Button("Search Twitter");
panel.add(searchButton);
final Label errorLabel = new Label();
panel.add(errorLabel);
panel.add(resultsPanel);
```

Now I can add the header, panel, and nav to the page specifically where I want them using `RootPanel.get`:

```
RootPanel.get("header_container").add(header);
RootPanel.get("nav_container").add(nav);
RootPanel.get("content_container").add(panel);
```

The app now has nice clean markup but no layout at all; just some unstyled divs. Now we can jump back into the CSS. For the desktop version we want the header on top, the navigation on the left, and the content in the center adjacent to the nav and below the header.

```
#header_container {
}
#nav_container {
    position: absolute;
    width: 10em;
    left: 0px;
    top: 4em;
}
#content_container {
    position: absolute;
```

```
        left: 11em;
        top: 4em;
    }
```

I left the header alone since it looks fine. For the nav and content containers I made them be absolutely positioned then hard coded a `width`, `left`, and `top` value. The navigation will be 10 ems wide and 4 em from the top of the page to make room for the header. The `content_container` div will be 11ems from the left to make room for the navigation, and also 4 ems down. Notice that I'm using em's instead of pixels. This makes sure the page scales nicely with the user's preferred font.

The above CSS is now the default. When the screen is narrower than 480px we want the layout to change. That's what this CSS does:

```
@media screen and (max-width: 480px) {
    #nav_container {
        width: 100%;
    }
    #content_container {
        top: 7em;
        left: 0em;
    }
    .nav .gwt-Button {
        width: auto;
        margin: 0.1em 0.5em 0.1em 0.5em;
    }

}
```

If the screen is narrower then the navigation will stretch completely across the screen using `width:100%`. The content moves further down and all the way to the left using `top: 7em` and `left:0em`. We also set the width of the navigation buttons to auto. Before they were 100% wide, meaning they would *each* be as wide as the screen. Instead we want them to be sized automatically based on the text in them, which is what `auto` does. I also tweaked the margins a tiny bit to make them look prettier. The final results on a phone look like Figure 4-4.

In all of this talk about screen size we have assumed that a particular device always has the *same size* but that's not always true. Many devices can actually be rotated using an accelerometer, which is the device equivalent of resizing the browser window. You can create conditional styles to deal with this by sticking with the width media selector. The width will usually be updated when the user rotates the device. If you want to do something special just for portrait or landscape mode, rather than depending on the screen width you can do it with these media selector:

```
@media all and (orientation:portrait) {
}
@media all and (orientation:landscape) {
}
```

CSS is incredibly powerful. It can restyle almost anything on the page using a very simple syntax and degrades gracefully. All web renderers will ignore any CSS properties

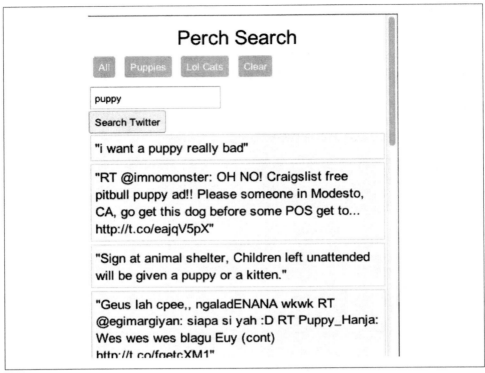

Figure 4-4. PerchSearch using the tags first approach.

they don't understand. This lets you add advanced features like animations for recent browsers and devices but still fall back gracefully to standard features on less sophisticated browsers.

Thanks to our tags first approach we can completely restyle the app without modifying code at all. This did require a bit of extra work to set up the tags , however. In the next chapter we will take a different approach to making apps ready for mobile.

CHAPTER 5

Building a Pure Mobile App with GWT Mobile UI

So far we have used GWT to build a standard desktop web app then optimized it for mobile using CSS tricks. This approach will work for many projects, especially if you are repurposing existing content. However, if you want to make an app that really *feels* native then you need something more.

Native mobile apps typically have touch centric controls like scrolling lists, large buttons, navigation tabs, and animated screen to screen transitions. We could build these from scratch in GWT by using a lot of hand written CSS and Java code, but why do that when there are already great libraries out there which will do the job for us. For the next project we will use one such library: GWT Mobile UI.

GWT Mobile UI is an open source collection of GWT widgets specifically designed for mobile devices. It has input widgets (buttons and sliders) as well as different panels for mobile style layouts. It also has a nice framework for animated transitions from one screen to the next. With this framework in our toolkit we can create a mobile app that feels completely native without having to reinvent the wheel.

For this project I'm going to build an app I've always wanted: a wine journal. My wife and I love to try different wines but I always forget which ones we liked and where we drank them. I own a paper wine journal but I always forget to bring it with me when we go out to eat. Sounds like a job for a mobile app.

Designing the Wine Journal

Before we start building the app let's plan what the app will look like. Upfront planning will ensure we have all of the pieces we need before starting to build it.

Feature List

The finished app will have the following features:

Wine List
> First we need a list of the wines I have tried. Mobile apps should to conserve space because mobile devices have small screens. The wine list should just show the name of the wine, the kind, and the rating.

Wine Details
> If you click on a wine in the list it should take you to a new screen which shows the full details of the wine: vineyard, where the wine was bought/drunk, a photo of the label, rating, etc.

Add Wine
> Initially the user won't have any wines, so they need a screen to add a new one. This should be a list of input fields for the name, variety, rating, etc. Since this is a mobile device which likely has a camera and GPS we should take advantage of device features whenever possible.

Navigation Choices

So that's it for the three main screens. We also need a way of navigating from one screen to another. Since looking at your list of wines is the most common thing someone will do the wine list should be the first screen you see when you start the app. That way you don't have to navigate anywhere to get to the most common thing.

To get to the wine details you just click on a wine. It would be nice to have some sort of transition to the wine details screen so the user has a sense of what is happening. Once you are on the wine details screen you need a way to get back, so there should be a back button at the top of the screen. You could put the back button anywhere, but the top left is the standard that most mobile devices are moving towards.

To get to the *add wine* screen we need an add button. The standard place for this is a header or footer containing action buttons. When you get to the add screen you should be able to have a button to actually complete adding the wine, and another for canceling. But where should these buttons go? I suggest the back button goes in the top left, just like on the wine details screen. This is a good place for it because it fits what other mobile apps do and is consistent with the wine details screen.

The add button could go in the upper right. Many apps do this, but I think it should go at the bottom below the entry fields. This has two advantages. First, you get to the add button right when you need it: after you've filled in the last field. Second, the add button will probably be hidden by the bottom of the screen until you have scrolled down far enough to fill out the form fields. This means it is hidden until you really need it. If the user accidentally gets to the add wine screen then the only action button they will immediately see is the back button, which is probably what they wanted. By carefully choosing where the action buttons go we have created a better user experience.

GWT Mobile UI

To use GWT Mobile UI we first need to get it. You can download the source from *here* and compile it by hand, or download the prebuilt jar from my website *here*. It is important to note that GWT jars aren't like regular jars. They contain more than just compiled Java classes. They also have the source that will be needed by the gwtc compiler to generate the JavaScript. They also have XML definitions for the entire library. This makes them a bit trickier to use but far more portable and encapsulated.

To add a 3rd party module to your project you have to update a few files. First, put the *gwtmobileui.jar* in a lib directory, then add it to your build script so that gwtc can find it. Open your `build.xml` file and go to the section that defines the `project.class.path` variable. It should be near the top of the file. Add a line referencing your new jar.

```
<path id="project.class.path">
    <pathelement location="war/WEB-INF/classes"/>
    ...
    <!-- Add any additional non-server libs (such as JUnit) -->
    <fileset dir="war/WEB-INF/lib" includes="**/*.jar"/>
    <pathelement location="lib/gwtmobile-ui-1.1.jar"/>
</path>
```

Now you need to add the functionality of this jar to your project. Remember from the earlier chapter that your project is a module defined by an XML file. Open this XML file, *MyFirstApp.gwt.xml* and add this line near the top:

```
<inherits name='com.google.gwt.user.User'/>
<inherits name='com.gwtmobile.ui.gwtmobile_ui'/>
```

This will import the GWT Mobile UI classes into your module. Finally, you may also need to tell your IDE to add the jar to your classpath if it isn't already aware of the GWT XML files. I use IntelliJ and had to manually add the jar to my classpath. With all of that in place we can start building the app.

Building the Screens

When we first created our app it generated a `MyFirstApp` class. This is the entry point that starts our application. GWT will initialize and create our first screen. Let's start by defining a new class called `Wine`. This is our data model. It will just have some public variables as properties. Since this class will never be exposed outside of the project I'm not worried about encapsulation. (Switching to getters and setters later is easy enough to do with refactoring tools, so let's not worry about it right now).

The Wine class looks like this:

```
public class Wine {
    public String name;
    public String variety;
    public int rating;
    public String vineyard;
}
```

For now we won't worry about storing the wines to long term storage. Let's just initialize some dummy data. Here is the `initWines()` method in MyFirstApp:

```
ArrayList<Wine> wines = new ArrayList<Wine>();

private void initWines() {
        Wine w1 = new Wine();
        w1.name = "foo wine";
        w1.variety = "resling";
        w1.rating = 3;
        w1.vineyard = "foo yard";
        wines.add(w1);

        w1 = new Wine();
        w1.name = "bar wine";
        w1.variety = "malbec";
        w1.rating = 2;
        w1.vineyard = "foo yard";
        wines.add(w1);
}
```

Wine List Screen

Now let's create a new class in a new file for the wine list. GWT really only thinks in terms of widgets whereas mobile apps usually have the concept of a page. The user can navigate from one page to another with transitions between them. When the user hits the back button it should go to the previous page, still in the state the user left it in. Because this is such as common metaphor the GWT Mobile UI library provides a Page class.

A Page is a panel containing widgets with a special goto method on it. You can call goto to go to any other page. If that page invokes the back method then the framework will automatically move back to the previous page. The framework handles all history management for you, along with automatic transitions between the pages. If even implements the transitions with CSS transforms so that the drawing will be hardware accelerated on many devices.

Our first page will simply list the wines. To show the list we will use a ListPanel. This is a class provided by GWT Mobile UI which draws very nice lists with large click targets.

```
public WineListPage(MyFirstApp mains) {
    this.main = mains;
```

```
        wineList = new ListPanel();
        wineList.setShowArrow(true);

        regenerateWineList();
    ...
    }
    public void regenerateWineList() {
        wineList.clear();
        for (Wine w : main.wines) {
            wineList.add(new Label(w.variety + ": " + w.name));
        }
    }
}
```

Notice the call to `wineList.setShowArrow(true)`. iOS set a standard for lists that are used for navigation. It shows that the list item will go somewhere by including an arrow at the end. The `ListPanel` will add these arrows for us automatically if we call `setSho wArrow(true)`.

To do the actual navigation we need an event handler to listen for the actual list item clicks. When the user clicks on an item we will create a wine details page for that item and navigate to it with goto.

```
wineList.setSelectable(true);
wineList.addSelectionChangedHandler(new SelectionChangedHandler() {
    public void onSelectionChanged(SelectionChangedEvent e) {
        Utils.Console("in a selection " + e.getSelection());
        goTo(new ViewWinePage(main.wines.get(e.getSelection())));
    }
});
```

In addition to the list, the first page also has a header showing the page you are on and including the button to add a new item. GWT Mobile UI has a class for this as well: `HeaderPanel`. HeaderPanel creates a very nice header with pretty integrated buttons. It also will remain fixed to the top of the screen even if the user scrolls down.

```
HeaderPanel header = new HeaderPanel();
header.setCaption("Yours Wines");
header.setRightButton("Add");
header.setRightButtonClickHandler(new ClickHandler() {
    public void onClick(ClickEvent clickEvent) {
        goTo(new AddWinePage(main));
    }
});
```

Notice that we've added a handler just for the right button. It also uses the goto method to go to the AddWinePage page

Finally to wrap it up we need a single HTML panel containing both the header and list. We also need to put the list inside of a ScrollPanel so that the wines will be scrollable.

```
panel = new HTMLPanel("div","");
panel.add(header);
ScrollPanel winescroll = new ScrollPanel();
winescroll.add(wineList);
```

```
panel.add(winescroll);
initWidget(panel);
```

If you comment out the event handlers (since they reference classes that we haven't actually created yet) then run the app on a phone it will look like Figure 5-1.

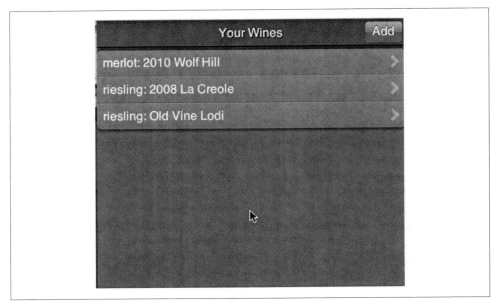

Figure 5-1. Wine list screen

Wine Details Screen

The wine details screen is very similar to the wine list screen. We have a header with a back button then a list panel containing the details of the wine. Here's the code for that

```
public ViewWinePage(Wine wine) {
    header = new HeaderPanel();
    header.setCaption("" + wine.name);
    header.setLeftButton("Back");

    scroll = new ScrollPanel();

    list = new ListPanel();
    ListItem item = null;

    item = new ListItem();
    item.add(new Label("Name: "));
    item.add(new Label(""+wine.name));
    list.add(item);

    item = new ListItem();
    item.add(new Label("Variety: "));
```

```
        item.add(new Label(""+wine.variety));
        list.add(item);

        item = new ListItem();
        item.add(new Label("Vineyard: "));
        item.add(new Label(""+wine.vineyard));
        list.add(item);

        scroll.add(list);

        panel = new VerticalPanel();
        panel.add(header);
        panel.add(scroll);
        initWidget(panel);
    }
```

Notice that I didn't define an event handler for the back button. That's because the UI framework is very smart. If you create a button with the text *back* it will automatically add an event handler to return to the previous item in the history stack. Here is what the wine details screen will look like Figure 5-2.

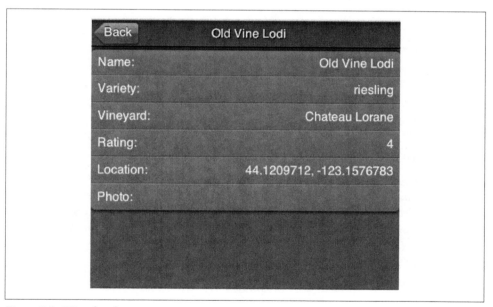

Figure 5-2. Wine details screen

The AddWinePage

The AddWinePage is a bit more complicated because it has several types of widgets. For each piece of wine info we have a list item. On the left side is a label with the name of the field. On the right side some sort of input widget. For fields which are pure free form text, like the name of the wine, we can just use a `TextBox`. For fields which can only have one of a few values, like the varieties of wines, we will use a `DropDownList`.

```
public AddWinePage(MyFirstApp mains) {
    this.main = mains;

    //add wine panel
    ListPanel addPanel = new ListPanel();

    ListItem nameRow = new ListItem();
    nameRow.add(new Label("Wine name:"));
    nameBox = new TextBox();
    nameRow.add(nameBox);
    addPanel.add(nameRow);

    ListItem vineyardRow = new ListItem();
    vineyardRow.add(new Label("Vineyard:"));
    vineyardBox = new TextBox();
    vineyardRow.add(vineyardBox);
    addPanel.add(vineyardRow);

    variety = new DropDownList();
    DropDownItem it1 = new DropDownItem();
    it1.setText("Riesling");
    it1.setValue("riesling");
    variety.add(it1);
    it1 = new DropDownItem();
    it1.setText("Merlot");
    it1.setValue("merlot");
    variety.add(it1);

    ListItem varietalRow = new ListItem();
    varietalRow.add(new Label("Varietal"));
    varietalRow.add(variety);
    addPanel.add(varietalRow);
```

I could have used a drop-down list for the rating, but the rating only has five possible values, to it made more sense to us a set of radio buttons. Then the user can just tap the button of the rating they want. The photo and location fields require special attention, so let's leave those blank for now. Here is what the add wine screen will look like Figure 5-3.

If you compile this app and put it on a web server then you can load it directly on your mobile device or desktop browser and it should work. So far we haven't used any device specific features so it works even without PhoneGap. The nice thing about this form of development is that we can build up the app incrementally and the code looks very similar to the final output. Plus we haven't had to do any custom styling yet. GWT Mobile UI took care of that for us.

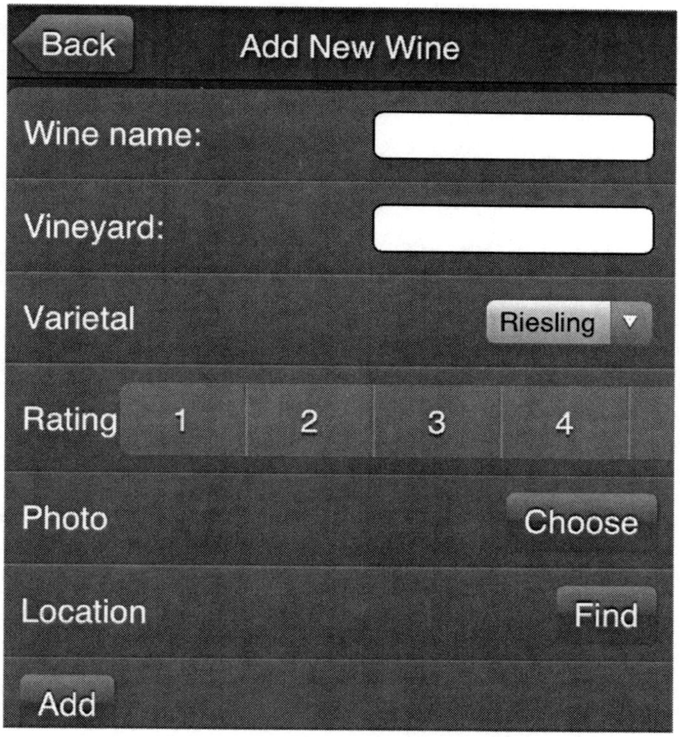

Figure 5-3. Add wine screen

Saving the Wine Data

The wine journal now lets the user add wines and view them, but we are only storing them in an ArrayList. This means the minute you restart the app all of the data will be gone. GWT provides a storage API to save data permanently on disk. The Storage API is actually a part of HTML 5. It is a key value store defined by the W3C and is now supported by most web browsers. This means GWT can support it natively without any special plugins.

Notice I said that the Storage API was a key-value store. This means the only thing it can store are key-value pairs of strings. It has no tables, schemas, or data types; just keys and values. Keys and values may seem limiting, but they are actually quite flexible. We just need a way to neatly convert our list of wines into a bunch of key value pairs. Start by thinking in reverse: how would we store a single wine object.

The wine object has several fields on it. For the name field we could store it with the key "name" and the actual wine.name field as the value. We could do the same for the variety: *variety*:wine.variety.

Now suppose we want to store two wines? Storing both wine names with the key *name* wouldn't work because the second wine would overwrite the first one. We need the two keys to be unique, and also associated with the actual wine object. We can do this by giving each wine an ID and using that ID as part of the key. Here's what the code would look like:

```
if(wine.id == null) {
    wine.id = "wine_"+Math.random();
}
storage.setItem(wine.id+"/name",wine.name);
storage.setItem(wine.id+"/variety",wine.variety);
```

I added an id field to the Wine class. If the id is currently unset (null) then it generates a new random id. Since Java's random numbers are quite large we can be confident that they will be unique. Then we store each field using the id+"/fieldname". Now we can store all of the fields in a unique and accessible way. Notice that since some of the fields are actually numbers instead of strings, I have prepended them with "" to turn them into strings.

Now that we have the wines stored we still need a way to store the IDs themselves so we can retrieve the wines later. We can do this by saving a list of the IDs separated by commas. This is the final code:

```
if(Storage.isSupported()) {
    Storage storage = Storage.getLocalStorageIfSupported();
    String ids = null;
    for(Wine wine : wines) {
        if(wine.id == null) {
            wine.id = "wine_"+Math.random();
        }
        storage.setItem(wine.id+"/name",wine.name);
        storage.setItem(wine.id+"/variety",wine.variety);
        storage.setItem(wine.id+"/vineyard",wine.vineyard);
        storage.setItem(wine.id+"/rating",""+wine.rating);
        storage.setItem(wine.id+"/geolat",""+wine.geoLat);
        storage.setItem(wine.id+"/geolon",""+wine.geoLon);
        storage.setItem(wine.id+"/photoURL",""+wine.photoURL);
        if(ids == null) {
            ids = wine.id;
        } else {
            ids += ("," + wine.id);
        }
    }
    storage.setItem("winekeys",ids);
}
```

Loading the wines when the app starts up is easy: just reverse the process of saving them. First we check if storage is supported. If it is then we get a reference to the local storage and get the wine keys. This is a list of ids separated by commas, so we can split them into an array of strings with the String.split[] command, then loop over the keys.

Here's what it looks like:

```
Storage storage = Storage.getLocalStorageIfSupported();

String winekeys = storage.getItem("winekeys");
if(winekeys == null) return;
String[] keys = winekeys.split(",");
for(String key : keys) {
    Wine wine = new Wine();
    wine.id = key;
    wine.name = storage.getItem(key+"/name");
    wine.variety = storage.getItem(key+"/variety");
    wine.vineyard = storage.getItem(key+"/vineyard");
    wine.photoURL = storage.getItem(key+"/photoURL");
    if(storage.getItem(key+"/rating") != null) {
        wine.rating = Integer.parseInt(storage.getItem(key+"/rating"));
    }
    if(storage.getItem(key+"/geolat") != null) {
        wine.geoLat = Double.parseDouble(storage.getItem(key+"/geolat"));
    }
    if(storage.getItem(key+"/geolon") != null) {
        wine.geoLon = Double.parseDouble(storage.getItem(key+"/geolon"));
    }
    wines.add(wine);
}
```

For each key the code above creates a new wine object then sets the fields by retrieving the values using the wine id. The numeric fields are converted from strings back into numbers.

Now that we have methods to load and save the wines we can call them from the appropriate places. initWines should be called just before showing the WineListPage in the MyFirstApp class. saveWines is called in the AddWineHandler of the AddWinePage.

Getting the User's Location

Everything we have done so far has used the regular APIs available in a desktop web browser. We have only used PhoneGap for its packaging tools. However, Phone Gap has some of its own APIs to access things that aren't available in the web browser such as the user's GPS location. (Some browsers now provide this feature as well, but Phone Gap provides a nice uniform API to access it on all mobile OSes).

To use the PhoneGap APIs we need a GWT wrapper library. Fortunately the same GWT Mobile project has Phone Gap wrappers. You can get the Phone Gap wrapper API from *here* as source or download the precompiled version from my site *here*. Add the jar to your project as before. Be sure to add it to the build.xml and your IDE, then edit your gwt.xml file to add this line:

```
<inherits name='com.googlecode.gwtphonegap.PhoneGap' />
```

Now you can call the PhoneGap APIs directly from Java code. First, you need to initialize Phone Gap. This sets up a bunch of internal API mappings and can take a significant amount of time depending on the platform. To deal with this Phone Gap provides a callback for when it is done being initialized. That's when we can safely start the rest of our app. Here's what the code looks like:

```java
phoneGap = GWT.create(PhoneGap.class);
phoneGap.addHandler(new PhoneGapTimeoutHandler() {
    public void onPhoneGapTimeout(PhoneGapTimeoutEvent event) {
        Utils.Console("phonegap failed to initialize");
    }
});
phoneGap.addHandler(new PhoneGapAvailableHandler() {
    public void onPhoneGapAvailable(PhoneGapAvailableEvent e) {
        initWines();
        wineListPage = new WineListPage(MyFirstApp.this);
        Page.load(wineListPage);
    }
});
phoneGap.initializePhoneGap();
```

Now that PhoneGap is initialized we can call the Location API. If you just want the current position the API is quite simple. Obtain the GeoLocation object from PhoneGap then call its getCurrentPosition method with a callback. The callback will be invoked when the user's current position becomes available. On some devices this could take several seconds if the GPS receiver is asleep or has not gotten a live satellite fix in a while. If the position can't be found for some reason then the callback's onFailure method will be called.

Once you get a valid position you can save it to be persisted along with the rest of the wine's info. This is all done inside the event handler for the Find button.

```java
Button locationButton = new Button();
locationButton.setText("Find");
locationButton.addClickHandler(new ClickHandler() {
    public void onClick(ClickEvent clickEvent) {
        Geolocation geo = main.phoneGap.getGeolocation();
        geo.getCurrentPosition(new GeolocationCallback() {
            public void onSuccess(Position position) {
                selectedPosition = position;
                locationLabel.setText("Location: " +
                        position.getCoordinates().getLatitude() +
                        ", " + position.getCoordinates().getLongitude());
            }
            public void onFailure(PositionError positionError) {
                Utils.Console("failure");
            }
        });
    }
});
locationRow.add(locationButton);
```

Taking Photos

Using the camera from PhoneGap is very similar to the GeoLocation API. You get a reference to PhoneGap's Camera object, then call getPicture with a callback. getPicture also requires an options object to configure how you want the picture taken. You can request the picture to come from a saved photo album instead of a live camera picture. You can also request that the photo be returned to you as either a URL or base64 encoded image data.

The code to get a photo as a URL from the live camera looks like this:

```
Button photoButton = new Button();
photoButton.addClickHandler(new ClickHandler() {
    public void onClick(ClickEvent clickEvent) {
        Utils.Console("clicked");
        PictureOptions options = new PictureOptions();
        options.setDestinationType(PictureOptions.DESTINATION_TYPE_FILE_URI);
        options.setSourceType(PictureOptions.PICTURE_SOURCE_TYPE_CAMERA);
        main.phoneGap.getCamera().getPicture(options, new PictureCallback() {
            public void onSuccess(String s) {
                Utils.Console("succeeded: " + s);
            }
            public void onFailure() {
                Utils.Console("failed");
            }
        });
    }
});
```

After adding the location and photo we need to update the wine saving and loading code. In the AddWineHandler add the following lines just before the call to saveWines()

```
wine.photoURL = photoURL;

// geo position
if(selectedPosition != null) {
    wine.geoLat = selectedPosition.getCoordinates().getLatitude();
    wine.geoLon = selectedPosition.getCoordinates().getLongitude();
}
selectedPosition = null;
main.wines.add(wine);
main.saveWines();
```

Then update saveWines and initWines to store and retrieve the new fields.

```
public void saveWines() {
...
    storage.setItem(wine.id+"/rating",""+wine.rating);
    storage.setItem(wine.id+"/geolat",""+wine.geoLat);
    storage.setItem(wine.id+"/geolon",""+wine.geoLon);
    storage.setItem(wine.id+"/photoURL",""+wine.photoURL);
...
}
private void initWines() {
...
```

```
        wine.photoURL = storage.getItem(key+"/photoURL");
        if(storage.getItem(key+"/geolat") != null) {
            wine.geoLat = Double.parseDouble(storage.getItem(key+"/geolat"));
        }
        if(storage.getItem(key+"/geolon") != null) {
            wine.geoLon = Double.parseDouble(storage.getItem(key+"/geolon"));
        }
    ...
```

Polish

To make this app look really nice on a phone there are a few more things we should
tweak. First we need to make the phone scale the content properly using a viewport
metatag. I've also added a few iOS-specific options to make it look nicer.

```
<!-- target-densityDpi is an Android-only viewport property.
    It sets viewport resolution. -->
<meta name="viewport"
    content="target-densityDpi=device-dpi, initial-scale=1.0, maximum-scale=1.0, user-
scalable=0"/>
<meta name="apple-mobile-web-app-capable" content="yes" />
<meta names="apple-mobile-web-app-status-bar-style" content="black-translucent" />
```

Finally we can have some control over the transitions. To jump from page to page we
have been using the goto method. This method also takes an optional *transition* argu-
ment to control how it will go from screen to screen. For example, to use a fade transition instead of a slide use the following code:

```
goTo(new ViewWinePage(main.wines.get(e.getSelection()))),
    Transition.FADE);
```

Next Steps

Now you have a fully functioning app that can work on virtually any mobile device.
This is just the beginning of the app, though. There are many more features you could
add, such as the ability to delete or edit existing wines and backing up the data to the
cloud. Consider what other info you could add automatically. The date and time the
user bought it? If they bought at a different time then they drank it? How many times
has the user drunk that wine?

If the app talks to a server you could do other interesting things like preload a list of
known existing wines for auto-completion, or let people share their favorite wines using
Facebook. From this basic app it is easy to continue adding new features and improve
the user experience.

CHAPTER 6

Advanced Mobile Optimizations

Optimizing the Experience

I often have developers ask me how to make a mobile version of their existing web or desktop app. The only answer I have is to simplify your interface. Mobile devices have less screen space, less CPU and memory, and the users are often on the go with little time for navigation. These would seem to be the obvious reasons for simplifying the interface, but reality is actually much more subtle.

Consider the following. Most websites are designed to entice the user. People come from all over and stumble across the website, perhaps via a search engine or Facebook link. The site must entice the user to stick around, try the features/services, and hopefully sign up; either by giving their email address or actually paying money for something. Websites are also used by returning users to actually use the services of the site. To deal with these different use cases websites become complex beasts, sometimes growing so large as to need the dreaded site map. If you need a sitemap then your design has utterly failed. A good interface *is* the sitemap.

In the mobile app arena things are a bit different. Sure, your app is a bit of a sales tool because it gives the user the best possible view of your services, but you don't have to do the initial sales pitch. If someone has downloaded your app then they have already made a decision to use your product, or at least give it a serious try. Installing an app is more of a commitment than loading a website. This means you can focus less on the sales pitch and more on the experience for returning users. In a sense *all* app users are returning users. This doesn't mean you should skip the help section, but it does mean you can focus more on what the user will actually do with your site/content/app.

Simplify, Simplify, Simplify

First, consider what someone actually wants to do with your content or app when they are on a mobile device. Anything that doesn't fit the primary use case should be scrapped. It sounds scary but you will find the end result is almost always worth it and crucial features can be restored later if you really need them. If you build your interface to focus on the primary use case you will always end up with something that user feels is actually more powerful. It can seem counter intuitive, but simpler things feel more powerful because the interface doesn't get in the way. Users can do what they want without anything holding them back.

Use defaults

Simplifying doesn't always mean removing features. Often it is a case of using good defaults. Interactions often require getting several pieces of information from the user. Can any of that information have useful defaults so the user doesn't have to enter it directly but rather approve it implicitly by not changing the default.

Use previous values

A previous value is just a default that the user already set before. Most apps let users repeat interactions. This is pretty much assumed since the user wouldn't have installed an app unless they really wanted to use it multiple times. Someone doesn't download a Twitter app to send a single tweet. They want to use it a lot. This means you should remember what the user does so you can do it again later. You can think of it as always leaving the app in the state the user left it. For example, in our wine app the user adds a wine including the choice of the type of wine: say, Merlot. When the user adds another wine consider leaving the selector set on Merlot. If they added one Merlot they may add another. That's one less thing the user has to type in. Navigation can live by this principle as well. If the user is in the add wine screen when they quit the app then the app should return to the add screen when launched again rather than jumping back to the main screen. Keep the app in the state the user last left it in.

Use device features

When asking the user for information, much of it could actually be gathered by querying the device instead of the user. Photo apps use the device orientation to tell if the image is a landscape or portrait photo rather than actually asking the user which way it is. What other information could you collect from the device instead of the user? Current date and time? GPS location? Compass direction?

Cat Mapper Example

Here is a real-life example. I built a mobile app to help the city of Portland track stray cats. Citizens can upload a photo of the cat and where the cat was seen, along with a few bits of information such as:

- Who owns the cat?
- Is the cat a stray?
- Have you seen the cat often?
- Is the cat fed inside or out?

This was originally a paper questionnaire that we were adapting to an app. By analyzing the paper form we were able to reduce the number of questions significantly, and increase the return rate and reliability of data.

First, we realized that the primary use case is the user taking a picture of a cat right in front of them and submitting it immediately to the cloud. This means we could use the current time and location rather than asking the user for the info. We also noticed that several of the questions were mutually exclusive. If the person was taking a picture of their own cat then they knew it wasn't a stray and knew if the cat was an indoor or outdoor cat and where the food was kept.

With this knowledge we divided workflow into two screens. First, you take a picture of the cat in front of you and click a button to say if this is your cat or someone else's. If it's your cat, we ask you questions about where the cat lives and eats. If it's a stray, we ask you questions about how often you see it and its apparent health. We don't ask you the question about how often you see it when it's your cat, since that is presumably very frequent.

Since this is a phone that we assume is online we could submit data straight to the server. This eliminated the need for local storage and an interface to manage it. There is also no setup because the server location never changes and all submissions are anonymous.

By dividing the workflow and using device information we reduced a 15-question form into an average five clicks. We were able to greatly simplify the interface through simple changes.

Other Ways to Simplify

Get rid of flair

> I know it's fun, but it wastes cycles and user time. Get rid of the splash screens. Jump straight into the app's main screen. If you need a splash screen for info on how to use the app, only show it the first time the user launches the app.

Get rid of gratuitous animation

> It seems fun the first time, but not the twentieth. Remember that an app is something the user will use over and over. Do keep animated transitions because they subconsciously let the user understand the app navigation, but keep them as minimal as possible. There is no need to use a cool 3D cube effect when a simple left/right slide transition would do just as well. This also is easier on the mobile CPU.

Use vertical space

> It's much easier for the hand to scroll down than left or right or click buttons. Rather than dividing a workflow into multiple screens consider putting everything in one long page with only one logical item per line. This is especially true when adapting web forms. Only do the actual screen transition when the user is affecting real (possibly undoable) change, such as submitting the form or ordering a product.

Flatten Your Menus

Drop down menus usually require a hover effect or need at least two clicks. They were designed for a mouse, not a finger. They should never be in mobile interfaces. Instead make your navigation one level. Even if your web/desktop menu has multiple levels, one level is better. To adapt it first remove features you won't need. Then if you still need multiple levels switch to a flattened hierarchy. This is when everything is at one level but still grouped together.

For example, suppose your interface lets the user choose from 50 movies to watch. The desktop version might have a two level menu. The first level is for the genre (action, comedy, horror, etc) then the second level lists the available movies in that genre. For mobile we can flatten this by still grouping them into the genres but putting them all in one list with some extra bit of information (like a prefix) to indicate the current genre.

This reduces the interaction to a single long screen that the user scrolls through rather than needing two clicks with a transition between screens.

Polish, Polish, Then Polish Some More

Though mobile apps feel easier to build because they are smaller and more focused than desktop sites/apps, they really need more polish for a couple of reasons. First, this app will be the primary way someone interacts with your content or service. They will use it over and over. That means any bugs or visual issues will *also* be seen over and over, and will get more annoying over time. Second, because an app is so much more focused and you've removed anything extraneous, the features which are left will come under more scrutiny. This all adds up to the need for more polish.

When you've done the first version of your mobile app, send it to as many beta testers as possible. Use mobile analytics systems like Google Analytics to see what people are actually doing with your app, then push out an update. Unlike desktop apps, mobile users accept and assume a much more frequent update cycle. Always be improving your app.

Be on the lookout for:

Text size
> Always make the largest text of your app or site (usually the headers) no more than 3× bigger than your body text.

Font selection
> Mobile devices typically don't have as many installed fonts as a desktop OS, and some don't font downloading. Choose two good sets of fonts. One set for body text and one for headers. Then make each kind cascade properly. This is a nice set that I often use:

```
h1, h2, h3, h4, h5 {
    font-family: Helvetica, Verdana, Arial, sans-serif;
    }

div, p {
    font-family: Georgia, "Times New Roman", Times, serif;
    }
```

In general I recommend a very vertical centric layout on mobile devices. Have a header or navigation, then **one** column of content, then a footer with further navigation. Keep the top navigation as minimal as possible. Let the user get to the content ASAP. On wider devices you can expose extra side columns, but keep the main content central.

Improving Download Time

Mobile devices often have slower network connections than desktops. They also have weaker CPUs which take longer to process downloaded data. This means download time is always a consideration, even if it's a locally installed app.

Media queries
> You can use media queries to control what assets are downloaded. If you are shipping your app as a mobile website instead of an app, then the queries can be very handy to only download mobile resources when viewed on a mobile device and larger ones for tablets and desktops. Don't use the query to overlay a set of mobile resources on top of the generic ones. This will result in the generic ones being downloaded and then discarded. Instead, make mobile be the default and overlay the desktop ones. Mobile first, then add others.

Don't assume that Photoshop and your other image editors produce the best PNGs
> Use a 3rd party image compressor like the open source pngcrush to re-encode your (still lossless) images with tighter compression. I have been amazed as the image savings possible. This matters even for installed apps because the user can install your app faster. Even after installation it matters because better compressed images can be loaded faster and take less memory at runtime.

Many visual components of your app can be done with CSS instead of images
> Instead of creating an image for every button use CSS gradients. Instead of pre-rendering drop shadows into graphics with Photoshop, use CSS box and text shadows. Use CSS `border-radius` instead of pre-rendering your rounded panels. Most of these CSS effects are GPU accelerated now and the CSS will usually require a lot less download time than the equivalent graphics.

Set up your web server to support gzip compression
> This is on the fly compression which most mobile browsers support. HTML and CSS are *extremely* compressible. You will sometimes get a factor of ten improvement.

Optimizing mobile applications is an art, not a science, and it changes over time as devices and networks improve. My best advice is to get your design right first, then optimize the performance and download time. No one wants to use an unusable design, no matter how fast it downloads. If the design looks great and is easy to use, then your customers will put up with a few extra seconds of download time.

CHAPTER 7

Box2D and Canvas

For the final project in this book we are going to make a game. Yes a real gosh darn pixel-powered game with cute characters and physics. The key here is HTML Canvas. Canvas is a 2D graphics API built into HTML 5. Virtually every modern browser has support for it, even the newest Internet Explorer, and pretty much every mobile device does as well. The devil is in the details, however. Canvas can be slow on mobile and not every device renders the same way. GWT hides some of this for us thanks to its Canvas wrapper but we will still need to carefully watch performance and platform bugs. But enough about canvas for the moment: let's design a game!

For this book I wanted to build a game that would really feel at home on a tablet. My favorite games as a kid were platformers. These are the games where a character jumps around to avoid obstacles and explore the world, sometimes collecting coins, power-ups, and defeating bad guys. Super Mario Bros is the definitive example of this kind of game.

Another advantage of choosing an older game style like a platformer is that they are a good match for the CPU constraints of a mobile device, and we can improve performance with graphics tricks that have been known for years. However nothing will fix one big glaring issue: platformers are meant to be played with buttons; either a D-pad on a Nintendo style controller or keys on a keyboard. Since most mobile devices either have neither a physical keyboard or D-pad, we will need a different kind of game input.

Though they don't have buttons, almost every phone now has an accelerometer. The accelerometer detects when the user has moved their device in any direction. Originally these were invented to detect sudden deceleration to trigger airbags in case of a car crash. The iPhone pioneered their use in a mobile device by using it to trigger screen rotation when the user moves from portrait to landscape mode. Now almost every mobile device has one.

If we used the accelerometer to tell which way is down then rather than moving the character around with arrow keys you could simply tilt the device to move the character in whichever direction is down. So rather than the character moving you are really moving the world *around* the character. Now we need a character that fits the idea of a *rolling downward* motion. A normal human like Indiana Jones would sort of work but it doesn't really make sense for him to be always walking down (unless he constantly slips on banana peels). Instead we can use a wheel or a ball, like the marble in the classic NES game Marble Madness.

For this game I chose a blob. He's a little rolling oil blob which moves and flows around. He can't move on his own so you must tilt the world to move him to where he needs to be. Instead of playing *as* the oil blob you are now the omnipotent player *guiding* the blob around. This is a perfect fit for accelerometer-based navigation.

So now that we have the game mechanic decided, let's draw up what the game would actually look like. My initial sketch of the level and concept is in Figure 7-1.

Figure 7-1. Initial blob game sketch

My vision is a level that you tilt *around* the blob. The blob himself is a black glob of oil that jiggles around with real physics so it's fun to make him run into things and bounce around like Jell-O. And of course he needs googly eyes. They make everything better. For the book I've only built one level of the game but it could easily be expanded to more.

Working with Canvas

First we need a way to draw on to the screen. Up until now everything we have done has been through GWT widgets that ultimately become buttons, DIVs, or other HTML

DOM elements on screen. This is great for business apps but a game needs the ability to draw pixels directly. This is where Canvas comes in.

Canvas is a new element added to HTML 5. It is essentially a rectangle in the page, much like a button or div, that lets you draw directly to it using functions like dra wRect and drawImage. With Canvas you get direct control over drawing to the screen, right down to the pixel level. While Canvas support varies from browser to browser; GWT provides a nice wrapper class called Canvas to smooth out the differences.

Let's get started by drawing some simple graphics. We will fill the background of the canvas with black then draw a red triangle in the middle.

```
canvasDraw = new CanvasDebugDraw(1024,700);

Canvas canvas = canvasDraw.getCanvas();
RootLayoutPanel.get().add(canvas);
```

Let's walk through it. The code above creates a new CanvasDebugDraw component. This is actually a wrapper around the real HTML DOM Canvas object. CanvasDebugDraw will be used to aid with debugging later. For now just know that we access the real canvas with getCanvas. Next we add the canvas as the root of the scene with Root LayoutPanel.get().add(canvas). Now we can draw something.

```
//get the context
Context2d ctx = canvas.getContext2d();

//fill the background
ctx.setFillStyle("black");
ctx.fillRect(0,0, canvasDraw.getWidth(), canvasDraw.getHeight());

//draw the triangle
ctx.setFillStyle("red");
ctx.beginPath();
ctx.moveTo(300, 300);
ctx.lineTo(500,350);
ctx.lineTo(350, 500);
ctx.lineTo(300, 300);
ctx.closePath();
ctx.fill();
```

First we get a drawing context to draw on to. We get this by calling canvas.getCon text2D(). In the future there may be other contexts, such as 3D, but for this book we will always use the 2D context. With this ctx object we can draw whatever we need. First the code clears the background by setting the fill style to black then calling fillRect with the size of the canvas. The next steps switch the fill style to red then creates a path for a triangle. After the shape is defined with closePath() we fill the shape with fill(). The result looks like Figure 7-2.

Canvas is a pretty simple immediate mode drawing API, similar to Java2D. This is no accident as they were both inspired by the PostScript drawing model, as were many other APIs such as PDF. All drawing is done by setting state variables, such as the current fill style or line width, setting geometry, and then finally calling a drawing

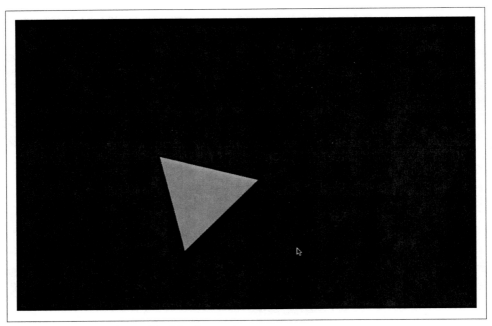

Figure 7-2. Red triangle on a black background

function like `fill`. Canvas only supports rectangles and paths. A path is a shape composed of lines, arcs, and curves. All other shapes, like a rounded rectangle or a star shape, must be drawn using a path.

Canvas also has many advanced features like as fonts, blending, and transformations. It is a big enough API to require a book of its own and is too much to cover here. Instead I will point you to the W3C Canvas spec and a hands on Canvas tutorial I wrote for OSCON 2011 (*http://projects.joshy.org/presentations/HTML/CanvasDeepDive/presentation.html*). It's a great intro which will take you from the basics of Canvas all the way through animation and pixel manipulation.

Physics with Box2D

Now that we know how to draw something we can create a simple world with a blob character. Drawing them will be easy since they are just a few filled shapes but making them *behave* like real objects takes a bit more. To actually make the blob flow and bounce off of walls in a realistic way we need real physics calculations. For simple two dimensional physics most games use the excellent open source physics simulation library Box2D (available at *http://www.box2d.org/*). It is written in C but has been ported to other languages. Fortunately someone has already ported it to GWT. All we have to do is hook it up.

Download GWT Box2D from *http://code.google.com/p/gwtbox2d/* . They don't provide prebuilt binaries so you'll need to compile it from scratch. Check out the source from *http://gwtbox2d.googlecode.com/svn/trunk/* with subversion. It requires Gradle to build. You can install Gradle by downloading it from *http://gradle.org/* and putting it in your path. Now go to the *box2d* dir and run *gradle* to download, compile, and install everything you need. It will use maven underneath so you will need that installed as well, which we already did for the wine journal application. Once it completes building it will produce a final `gwtbox2d-core-1.0-SNAPSHOT.jar`. Add this jar to your build.xml for GWT to find it, and also in your IDE's classpath if you are using an IDE. Or you can skip all of that compiling nonsense and download the precompiled jar from the website that accompanies this book.

Using Box2D is a bit more complex than simply drawing shapes. We have to create objects for each thing in our world, describe where they are and how they behave, then give them to Box2D to manage. Let's start with something simple: a circle dropping onto a line. Box2D has a few concepts that you must understand to use it, so we'll walk through them step by step.

The code below defines the world. Everything in Box2D exists inside the world and there is only one world.

```
//setup the world
Vec2 gravity = new Vec2(0, -10f);
world = new World(gravity, true);
world.setDebugDraw(canvasDraw);
canvasDraw.setCamera(0f, 10f, 20f);
```

First we create a new `World` object and save a reference to it. The World constructor takes a `Vec2` object, which is just an x and y pair. This vector defines the direction and amount of gravity. For now we will set it to `0,10`, which is roughly equivalent to real gravity on Earth at sea level. Next attach the world to the `canvasDraw` component. The canvasDraw will do basic drawing for us, which will help us later on for debugging. Finally set the camera for the canvasDraw. This setting means that the camera is centered at 0,10 with a size of 20f. These settings only matter during debug drawing which we will turn off later, so just stick with these defaults.

Now that we have a world, let's give it a floor:

```
//create a floor
BodyDef bodyDef = new BodyDef();
bodyDef.position.set(0.0f, 0.0f);
ground = world.createBody(bodyDef);
PolygonShape sd = new PolygonShape();
sd.setAsBox(10, 1, new Vec2(0,0), 0f);
ground.createFixture(sd, 0f);
```

Every object in Box2D is called a body. To define a body you need a body definition or bodydef. The bodydef defines the position and angle of the body, as well as other properties like mass, density, and starting velocity. For this example we will just set the position to 0,0 and leave the others with their default values. Then we pass the bodydef to the `world.createBody` method. What it returns is the real body. Remember, the bodydef was just a *definition*. Think of it as a template or factory for creating bodies. Once the body is created you can throw the definition away or reuse it to define more bodies (perhaps you need a bunch of similar ones).

With the body created now we can make a real box. First we create a PolygonShape and call `setAsBox` with a width, height, and position. Note that the position refers to the *center* of the box, not its upper left corner. Instead of using setAsBox we could use multiple lines to define a shape, but for anything rectangular the box will be more efficient.

With a shape we can now pass it to the `createFixture()` method of the body to create a *fixture*. I realize this sounds confusing. Which is the actual object: the body or the fixture? In a sense both are. A body is something which exists in the world and can be moved or rotated. A fixture is a part of the body which actually has a shape and other things can bounce against. If you want just a block then you would have a body with a single fixture on it in the shape of a rectangle. However, bodies can have multiple fixtures. You could define an L shape using one body with two fixtures next to each other.

Fixtures are often but not always adjacent to each other, forming a single shape, but they can be disconnected as well. So when should you group your fixtures in a single body and when should they be separate? The important thing to remember is that everything in a body moves together. You should use one body per *thing* in your game. Later on we will create an entire level that is a single body with lots of fixtures in it, some connected and some not. This works because the level itself, the walls and floors, is a single *thing* in our game. However, if we had something that moved on its own, like a drawbridge or a tower that could crumble, then that would need to be composed of fixtures in their own body.

Note that `createFixture` does return an object for the created fixture but I'm not saving it because I don't care about the object once it's created. Again, like bodydef, the PolygonShape is just a definition. Once the fixture is created I can throw away `sd` or reuse it to create more fixtures.

Now that we have our shape, how do we actually draw it on screen. Fortunately this is pretty easy. Any game boils down to a loop. Update the objects, draw them, then repeat. We can do this in GWT with a Timer set for the framerate we want:

```
renderTimer = new Timer() {
    @Override
    public void run() {
        step();
        step();
        step();
        render();
    }
};
renderTimer.scheduleRepeating(1000/30);
```

In this case we set the timer to repeat 30 times per second. To use the timer we override its run method to call step and render. Step looks like this:

```
public void step() {
    float timeStep = 1 / 30f;
    world.setWarmStarting(true);
    world.setContinuousPhysics(true);
    world.step(timeStep, 4, 3);
}
```

The step function makes the physics engine turn the crank each time it is called. This is where the actual physics calculations are done. Each time through we have the engine move everything a tiny bit for that slice of time. The various parameters affect how accurate the simulation is and how long the time step should be. Leave the defaults for now.

```
public void render() {
    canvasDraw.clear();
    canvasDraw.setFlags(DebugDraw.e_shapeBit + DebugDraw.e_jointBit);
    world.drawDebugData();
}
```

Rendering is actually quite easy because the canvasDraw debugging object we allocated earlier will do it for us. Just clear it, set some flags, then call world.drawDebugData. The flags define what things should be drawn. We want to see just the shapes and joints (I'll explain joints in a second). If we wanted to we could render the frames per second and many of other things but for now this is fine.

Notice in the loop code above we are calling step three times for every render. This is because we want our physics to be more accurate. If we care more about performance (as we will later one) then we can call it twice or even only once per rendering frame. This is one way to balance speed vs accuracy.

If you run the code as is, it will look like Figure 7-3.

It's not very interesting, but it does at least draw something. Now let's add an object that will move: a falling circle.

```
//create a circle
bodyDef.position.set(0,10);
bodyDef.type = BodyType.DYNAMIC;
Body circle = world.createBody(bodyDef);
CircleShape circleDef = new CircleShape();
circleDef.m_radius = 3f;
circle.createFixture(circleDef, 1f);
```

This code is very similar to the definition of the floor, with a few important differences. First, the bodydef's type is set to DYNAMIC. This lets Box2D know that the object will actually be able to move. Without that the circle would never fall. The shape is a circle, similar to the polygon for the floor, however createFixture is called with the circle plus the number 1. Before it was 0. This second parameter represents the density of the object. I left it as 0 for the floor because the floor will never move, so it won't matter.

Figure 7-3. A simple world simulation with Box2D

For the circle I set it to the standard density of 1. You can tweak these numbers later on to affect how fast your objects move and how bouncy they are.

With the new code in place the circle will show up on screen and fall down to hit the ground, as shown in Figure 7-4.

Figure 7-4. A falling circle.

Building the Game Level

Now let's build the real game. In the interest of time I won't show all of the code, just the important parts. First we need a bunch of boxes to represent the floors and walls of the level. We create them just as before, and each time I'm reusing the sd object, only changing the size and adding it as a fixture each time. This works because sd is a template; we can use it over and over.

```
PolygonShape sd = new PolygonShape();


BodyDef bd = new BodyDef();
bd.position.set(0.0f, 0.0f);
ground = m_world.createBody(bd);

//bottom edge
sd.setAsBox(71.0f, 0.4f, new Vec2(48.5f,-5), 0f);
ground.createFixture(sd, 0f);
//top edge
sd.setAsBox(60.0f, 0.4f, new Vec2(-5,26), 0f);
ground.createFixture(sd, 0f);
//left edge
sd.setAsBox(0.4f, 40.0f, new Vec2(-23.0f, 29.5f), 0.0f);
ground.createFixture(sd, 0f);
//right edge
sd.setAsBox(0.4f, 28.0f, new Vec2(120.0f, 22.5f), 0.0f);
ground.createFixture(sd, 0f);

sd.setAsBox(60.0f, 0.4f, new Vec2(60,50), 0f); ground.createFixture(sd, 0f);
sd.setAsBox(90.0f, 0.4f, new Vec2(55,70), 0f); ground.createFixture(sd, 0f);
sd.setAsBox(0.4f, 80f, new Vec2(140,0), 0f); ground.createFixture(sd, 0f);
sd.setAsBox(120.0f, 0.4f, new Vec2(45,-30), 0f); ground.createFixture(sd, 0f);
sd.setAsBox(0.4f, 80f, new Vec2(-60,0), 0f); ground.createFixture(sd, 0f);

//ramp
bd.position.set(60f,1f);
bd.angle = 10f;
ramp = m_world.createBody(bd);
sd.setAsBox(10.0f, 0.4f, new Vec2(0,0f), 0f);  ramp.createFixture(sd, 0f);
```

Note that the last block looks slightly different. It is a ramp so in addition to giving it a position and box size, I also set the angle in degrees.

Building a Blob with Joints

The blob character is more complicated than a circle or box. It moves as a unit but it also is composed of many little pieces which shift around a bit relative to each other. To build this we will use a structure called a *joint*. A joint represents multiple bodies stuck together in a particular way. In this case we will use a ConstantVolumeJointDef in the variable *blob*. It will let the bodies move around but still be attached to each other.

```
//create the blob structure
blob = new ConstantVolumeJointDef();

float cx = 0.0f;
float cy = 10.0f;
float rx = 5.0f;
```

```
float ry = 5.0f;
int nBodies = 10; //number of points in the blob field
float bodyRadius = 0.5f;
for (int i = 0; i < nBodies; ++i) {
    float angle = MathUtils.map(i, 0, nBodies, 0, 2 * 3.1415f);
    BodyDef bd = new BodyDef();
    bd.fixedRotation = true;

    float x = cx + rx * (float) Math.sin(angle);
    float y = cy + ry * (float) Math.cos(angle);
    bd.position.set(new Vec2(x, y));
    bd.type = BodyType.DYNAMIC;
    Body body = m_world.createBody(bd);

    FixtureDef fd = new FixtureDef();
    CircleShape cd = new CircleShape();
    cd.m_radius = bodyRadius;
    fd.shape = cd;
    fd.density = 1.0f;
    fd.filter.groupIndex = -2;
    body.createFixture(fd);
    blob.addBody(body);
    blobBodies.add(body);
}

blob.frequencyHz = 5.0f;
blob.dampingRatio = 0.5f;
m_world.createJoint(blob);
```

The code above looks complicated but it's actually pretty simple. We are going to create N circles arranged in a circle around a central point (cx and cy). Each time through the loop it creates a bodydef, does a bit of math to determine the location of the body, then creates a circle fixture for that body. Finally it adds each body to the blob as well as a list blobBodies for later bookkeeping.

After the loop, with the joint set up, it creates the real joint with createJoint(). Now have a joint with N bodies inside of it. Note the settings of frequencyHz and dampingRatio. All of the bodies in the joint are sort of stuck together by springs (or you can think of them as being embedded in jelly). Those two parameters control how quickly they will bounce around relative to each other. You can tweak these parameters to make the blob more or less bouncy, and control how jittery the oscillations are. You will find that in physics games there aren't a lot of hard and fast rules. We aren't trying to program the moon lander here; we just want something that *feels* right. You will spend a lot of time tweaking the settings and play testing until it feels perfect.

With the blob and walls in place it will look like Figure 7-5.

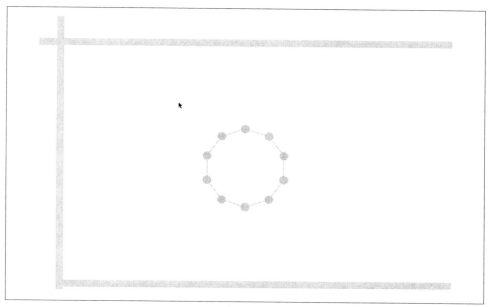

Figure 7-5. Blob and walls with debug drawing

Drawing the World

Now we want to actually draw the shapes ourselves instead of using `debugDraw`. This is all straightforward drawing code but somewhat verbose. First, comment out the debug drawing. Next draw the parts of the ground (really the entire level) by looping through the fixtures. Box2D uses a strangely sequenced API due to its C-based origin. Rather than returning an array or list you get the first object in a list and call getNext on it to loop through the items.

```
private void drawBorders(Context2d ctx) {
    Fixture fixtures = ground.getFixtureList();
    while(fixtures != null) {
        PolygonShape poly = (PolygonShape) fixtures.getShape();
        fillPoly(ctx,poly,"yellow","black");
        fixtures = fixtures.getNext();
    }
}

private void fillPoly(Context2d ctx, PolygonShape poly, String fillColor, String
strokeColor) {
    ctx.setFillStyle(fillColor);
    ctx.setStrokeStyle(strokeColor);
    ctx.beginPath();
    for(int i =0; i<poly.getVertexCount(); i++) {
        Vec2 v = poly.getVertex(i);
        if(i == 0) {
```

```
                ctx.moveTo(v.x,v.y);
            } else {
                ctx.lineTo(v.x,v.y);
            }
        }
        ctx.closePath();
        ctx.fill();
        //ctx.setLineWidth(0.2);
        //ctx.stroke();
    }
```

For each fixture we get the underlying shape and call `fillPoly`. Fill poly is a utility method which draws a polygon using the requested color. It sets the colors then builds a path with the vertexes of the poly, then calls fill.

Drawing the ramp is the same as the floor and walls, except that we must remember to rotate and translate the graphics to match the real object.

```
    private void drawRamp(Context2d ctx) {
        ctx.save();
        ctx.translate(ramp.getPosition().x,ramp.getPosition().y);
        ctx.rotate(ramp.getAngle());
        Fixture fixtures = ramp.getFixtureList();
        while(fixtures != null) {
            PolygonShape poly = (PolygonShape) fixtures.getShape();
            fillPoly(ctx,poly,"yellow","black");
            fixtures = fixtures.getNext();
        }
        ctx.restore();
    }
```

Now we get to the blob. We could just draw the blob as a bunch of circles, which is what it really is, but it wouldn't look as blobby. Instead I want to make a path which goes from the center of each circle in order, creating a wobbly polygon.

```
    private void drawBlob(Context2d ctx) {

        //draw the blob
        ctx.setFillStyle("black");
        ctx.beginPath();

        Body prev = blobBodies.get(blobBodies.size()-1);
        ctx.moveTo(prev.getPosition().x,prev.getPosition().y);

        //add a path segment for each body
        for(int i=0; i<blobBodies.size(); i++) {
            Body body = blobBodies.get(i);
            Body next = blobBodies.get((i+1) % blobBodies.size());
            Vec2 p = body.getPosition();
            Vec2 pp = prev.getPosition();
            Vec2 pn = next.getPosition();
            double ap = calcAngle(p,pp);
            double an = calcAngle(p,pn);

            Vec2 cp = calcPoint(p, ap, 0.1);
```

```
                Vec2 cn = calcPoint(p, an, -1);
                ctx.bezierCurveTo(
                        pp.x,pp.y,
                        cn.x,cn.y,
                        p.x,p.y);
                prev = body;
            }

            ctx.closePath();
            ctx.stroke();
            ctx.fill();

            //draw the eyeballs
            ctx.setFillStyle("white");
            float threshold = 0.2f;
            if(prevCenterX < centerX - threshold) {
                prevCenterX =  centerX -threshold;
            }
            if(prevCenterX > centerX + threshold) {
                prevCenterX = centerX + threshold;
            }
            if(prevCenterY < centerY - threshold) {
                prevCenterY =  centerY -threshold;
            }
            if(prevCenterY > centerY + threshold) {
                prevCenterY = centerY + threshold;
            }
            fillCircle(ctx,prevCenterX,prevCenterY,1.5f,"white");
            fillCircle(ctx,prevCenterX+2,prevCenterY,1.5f,"white");
            fillCircle(ctx, centerX, centerY, 0.7f, "black");
            fillCircle(ctx,centerX+2,centerY,0.7f,"black");

        }
```

For production I've changed the code a bit to use curves instead of straight lines and added some eyeballs. The final result looks like Figure 7-6.

The last step is to change gravity so that the blob will actually move. To do this we must respond to real input. For testing in the browser, since desktop browsers don't usually support the accelerometer, I've made a click handler. If you click anywhere on the screen it will change the gravity vector to point to where you clicked, relative to the center of the board.

```
    //event handlers
    public void onMouseDown(MouseDownEvent mouseDownEvent) {
        Vec2 gravity = new Vec2(
                (mouseDownEvent.getClientX()-canvasDraw.getWidth()/2)/30f,
                -(mouseDownEvent.getClientY()-canvasDraw.getHeight()/2)/30f
                );
        m_world.setGravity(gravity);
    }
```

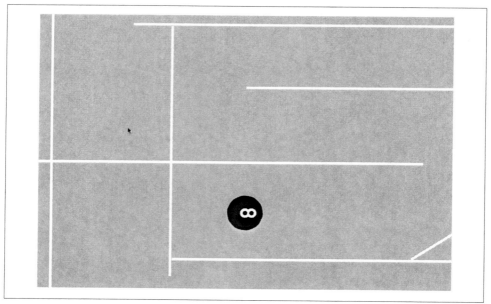

Figure 7-6. Blob and walls with real drawing

I also added code to make the world scroll as the blob moves around. It does this by calculating the current center of the blob and translating the graphics by the reverse of that amount on every frame before drawing the objects.

```
private void calcCenter() {
    float totalX = 0;
    float totalY = 0;
    for(Body body : blobBodies) {
        totalX += body.getPosition().x;
        totalY += body.getPosition().y;
    }
    prevCenterX = centerX;
    prevCenterY = centerY;
    centerX = (totalX/((float)blobBodies.size()));
    centerY = (totalY/((float)blobBodies.size()));
    //logger.info("center = " + centerX + " " + centerY);
}
```

Hooking Up the Accelerometer

Now that our game works we need to put it on a mobile device. We will do this just as before, using PhoneGap. To make the game tilt we need to access the accelerometer. PhoneGap lets you listen for acceleration events using the watchAcceleration call.

```
final PhoneGap phoneGap = GWT.create(PhoneGap.class);
phoneGap.addHandler(new PhoneGapAvailableHandler() {
    public void onPhoneGapAvailable(PhoneGapAvailableEvent event) {
```

```
            AccelerationOptions options = new AccelerationOptions();
            options.setFrequency(50);
            phoneGap.getAccelerometer().watchAcceleration(options,new
AccelerationCallback() {
                public void onSuccess(Acceleration acceleration) {
                    Vec2 gravity = new Vec2((float)-acceleration.getY()*10f,
(float)acceleration.getX()*10f);
                    m_world.setGravity(gravity);
                }
                public void onFailure() {
                    logger.severe("accell failed: ");
                }
            });
        }
    });
```

The code above creates a new AccelerationOptions() object and sets the frequency to 50. The frequency determines how often the current acceleration will be returned. Since this is for a real time game I have set it to 50. For other kinds of applications a lower value may be used. Each time the acceleration is returned the code sets a new gravity value based on the current X and Y of the acceleration. This represents the direction that gravity is currently pointing.

Now the game can be put on a real device using the PhoneGap build system, the same as in previous chapters. To make this feel more like a real game I added a splash screen and a goal at the end of the level. When the player reaches this goal it will show a "You've won" screen. Future versions of this game could add more levels and different obstacles.

Next Steps

Congratulations! You've finished reading the book. By this point you can build GWT applications that run on iOS, Android, and webOS devices. But this is only the beginning. PhoneGap and GWT are both rich ecosystems full of 3rd party libraries. They are also both under active development and will gain new features over time. Here are a few libraries and tools you might want to investigate:

GWT Eclipse Plugin

If you are an Eclipse user, you definitely want to install the GWT Plugin for Eclipse. It gives you a wonderful integrated GWT experience with debugging tools, easy deployment to the Google App Engine, and a GWT visual UI designer. See *http:// code.google.com/eclipse/*.

GWT-Sound

SoundManager 2 is a cross-platform sound API that uses HTML 5 audio, works around platform differences, and falls back gracefully to Flash when available. GWT Sound is a wrapper around the SoundManager API. See *http://www.schill mania.com/projects/soundmanager2/* and *http://code.google.com/p/gwt-sound/*.

GWT-Voices

Another sound API for GWT. Recommended by my GWT friends. See *http://code .google.com/p/gwt-voices/*.

GWT Client Bundle Developer's Guide

GWT optimizes the generated JavaScript of your application when it does its full compile. The ClientBundle interface lets the GWT compiler optimize resources in your application as well, such as CSS, images, and language translations. The developer guide covers everything you need to know, including how to inline binary resources to speed up download time. See *http://code.google.com/webtoolkit/doc/ latest/DevGuideClientBundle.html*.

M-GWT

M-GWT is an awesome mobile toolkit for GWT that offers pixel-perfect iOS and Android UI emulation. This toolkit was very new when I started writing this book

but has come a long way. I highly recommend checking it out. See *http://www.m
-gwt.com/*.

Play N

Play N is a cross-platform game library for GWT. Not only does it have APIs
specifically for games, it can cross-compile to Flash and native Android apps as
well as HTML. It has even been used to port Angry Birds to Chrome OS. See *http:
//code.google.com/p/playn/*.

About the Author

Joshua Marinacci first tried Java in 1995 at the request of his favorite TA and never looked back. He has spent the last fifteen years writing Java user interfaces for wireless, web, and desktop platforms. After cowriting *Swing Hacks* with Chris Adamson, Joshua spent five years at Sun working on Java user interfaces full-time, contributing to Swing, NetBeans, JavaFX, and the Java Store. Then he explored the mobile web for two years as a developer advocate for webOS and has recently joined Nokia as a researcher.

Joshua holds a BS in computer science from Georgia Tech and lives in Eugene, Oregon, with his wife and baby son.

Get even more for your money.

Join the O'Reilly Community, and register the O'Reilly books you own. It's free, and you'll get:

- $4.99 ebook upgrade offer
- 40% upgrade offer on O'Reilly print books
- Membership discounts on books and events
- Free lifetime updates to ebooks and videos
- Multiple ebook formats, DRM FREE
- Participation in the O'Reilly community
- Newsletters
- Account management
- 100% Satisfaction Guarantee

Signing up is easy:

1. **Go to: oreilly.com/go/register**
2. **Create an O'Reilly login.**
3. **Provide your address.**
4. **Register your books.**

Note: English-language books only

To order books online:
oreilly.com/store

For questions about products or an order:
orders@oreilly.com

To sign up to get topic-specific email announcements and/or news about upcoming books, conferences, special offers, and new technologies:
elists@oreilly.com

For technical questions about book content:
booktech@oreilly.com

To submit new book proposals to our editors:
proposals@oreilly.com

O'Reilly books are available in multiple DRM-free ebook formats. For more information:
oreilly.com/ebooks

O'REILLY®

Spreading the knowledge of innovators | oreilly.com

©2010 O'Reilly Media, Inc. O'Reilly logo is a registered trademark of O'Reilly Media, Inc. 00000

Have it your way.

O'Reilly eBooks

- Lifetime access to the book when you buy through oreilly.com
- Provided in up to four DRM-free file formats, for use on the devices of your choice: PDF, .epub, Kindle-compatible .mobi, and Android .apk
- Fully searchable, with copy-and-paste and print functionality
- Alerts when files are updated with corrections and additions

oreilly.com/ebooks/

Safari Books Online

- Access the contents and quickly search over 7000 books on technology, business, and certification guides
- Learn from expert video tutorials, and explore thousands of hours of video on technology and design topics
- Download whole books or chapters in PDF format, at no extra cost, to print or read on the go
- Get early access to books as they're being written
- Interact directly with authors of upcoming books
- Save up to 35% on O'Reilly print books

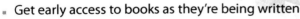 

See the complete Safari Library at safari.oreilly.com

Spreading the knowledge of innovators.   oreilly.com

©2011 O'Reilly Media, Inc. O'Reilly logo is a registered trademark of O'Reilly Media, Inc. 00000

RECEIVED

AUG 1 3 2013

ENGINEERING LIBRARY

CPSIA information can be obtained at www.ICGtesting.com
Printed in the USA
BVOW081035260312

286062BV00004B/7/P

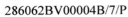

9 781449 308230